LAMB'S TALES

— ANOTHER WAG —

LAMB'S TALES

— ANOTHER WAG —

GREGOR LAMB

Published and printed by The Orcadian Limited, (Kirkwall Press),
Hell's Half Acre, Hatston, Kirkwall, Orkney, KW15 1DW, Scotland.
Telephone 01856 879000
Fax 01856 879001
www.orcadian.co.uk

ISBN 1-902957-21-0

Dedicated to the memory of Eileen Lamb
who did so much to care for others

ACKNOWLEDGEMENTS

I should like to thank all those Orcadians who, unwittingly or otherwise, have contributed to this collection of tales. I can usually attach a name to a story but in a few instances I have forgotten. I do remember and should particularly like to Len Wilson, Kirkwall; Margarets Flaws, Wyre; Karl Cooper, Holm; Harald Esson, Dounby; Alan James, Birsay; Neil Budge, Kirkwall; Mina Merriman, Sandwick; Susan Leonard, Stenness; Alan Watson, Kirkwall; Alastair Marwick, Birsay; Dupre Strutt, Kirkwall; Ronald Wishart, Stenness; Dave Holden, Somerset; Margaret Grant, Worcester; Bobby Leslie, Kirkwall; Steve Bichan, Deerness; Ernie Carter, New Zealand; Thora Linklater, Stenness; Bert Sinclair, Kirkwall; Ian Blair, Oxford and Walt Custer, USA. Thanks too to the former pupils of Stenness Primary School - now grown men and women. Did they ever imagine that some little incident in their early years would be recorded for posterity! Some of my contributors are no longer with us. I am the last of a big family and the humour of my mother, brothers and sisters is echoed throughout the book. I should like to mention especially Freddy Linklater of Stenness who had an enormous collection of humorous tales and whose passing I greatly regret. After a terrible illness he retained his sense of humour right to the end. When a friend called one morning to ask how he was he replied, 'Ah'm dyan min bit apert fae that Ah'm aalright.' We hope that Freddy's tales and the tales of others help to light up your life a little.

Gregor Lamb

The author's and publishers' royalties from this book will be shared by
Macmillan (Orkney) and Orkney MS Therapy Centre

ANOTHER WAG . . .

In Volume I we told the story of the Sanday mason who used to spit down the wall to check that his work was plumb. Such a method could not have been very reliable in windy Orkney! There must have been some 'cowboy' joiners around in those days too but perhaps the story told about one particular joiner was a little exaggerated. A joiner was well known for his shoddy work and rarely used a measure. One day he and his apprentice were renovating a house. The joiner came walking through the building with his hands held out in front of him, the palms in a vertical position. Brushing the apprentice aside he said, 'Oot o me wey beuy, Ah'm just the measure o a door.'

A pullet in Orkney dialect is an *arroo*. It is one of the few words in our dialect which has its origin in the Gaelic language. The original Gaelic is *eireag*. During the lst. World War, there were many appeals for all kinds of things and collectors went from house to house gathering what they could for the war effort and no questions were asked. This background has to be understood to appreciate the following misunderstanding:

When, at the end of that war, the poppy appeal was begun, a collector called at a house in Evie. A somewhat deaf old lady appeared at the door and the conversation went like this:-

'Ah'm collectan for Earl Haig's.'

'Oh Ah'm no sure if I hiv any bit Ah'll go and see.'

She returned after a short time and offered the collector some small hens' eggs.

The confused collector, realising that she had been misunderstood called out, 'Ah'm collectan for Earl Haig's.'

'Mercy,' replied the wife, 'I thowt thoo said thoo wir collectan arroo eggs.'

Auntie Sarah was a teacher and quite 'proper spoken.' She telephoned her sister one day and her niece took the call.

'This is Auntie Sarah,' she said, 'could I speak to your mother please?'

The little girl ran to fetch her mother shouting, 'Somebody caaled Andy Shaerer wants yi on the 'phone.'

A popular pastime among some of the boys at Stromness Academy in the 1950s was to go down to the public library at lunch-time. At that time the librarian was a fine old man by the name of Peter Esson who had many a story to tell. On one occasion he told us of a remarkable coincidence.

Peter had been in the trenches in the 1st World War. Parcels used to arrive regularly from Britain distributed by the Red Cross and the contents were handed out at random by their field officers. One day Peter was lucky enough to be given a parcel which he opened with great excitement and he was delighted to find in it a pair of hand-knitted socks. It was just the thing he needed for the cold nights he experienced there. That same day as he was putting them on he thought he felt something inside one of the socks. He took it off again. Sure enough, inside was a piece of paper. Peter will finish the story.

'I hid a luk at the piece o paeper and couldna believe me eyes. Written on hid wis the name and address o the wife that hid knitted the socks. The wife lived just twa-three doors along the street fae me in Stromness!'

Getting together for a few glasses of home-brewed ale was a common practice in some Orkney houses. As the night wore on some of the less inebriate members of the group would play tricks on those who had imbibed a little too much. There was a lot of hubbub and laughter in the kitchen of a farm in Firth and when the wife o the hoose who had been in the back keetcheen came through she wondered what the strange smell was in the air. One of the party pointed to the open fire and declared, 'Thee man is aalwis complainan aboot cowld feet so Ah'm pitten his beuts on the fire' – and the blue flames of the fine peat clods were spiralling up around them! It was rather a stupid trick to play on his generous host. The following trick was in slightly better taste.

A Stromness farmer was very fond of a drink. One night he called on a like minded neighbour and was liberally supplied with ale. After some hours of heavy drinking he said he would have to go outside for he was 'feelan seek.' He struggled to his feet, took out his false teeth, laid them on the table and with the help of the wall made his way outside. Meanwhile his host who had a better capacity for ale decided he would play a trick on him and opening the dresser drawer he withdrew an old set of false teeth which he dipped in the ale and quickly substituted for the set on the table. John (we'll call him) returned, ashen faced and slowly taking up his place at the table put the false teeth in his mouth. The family looked at him with bated breath while he struggled to get the teeth to fit. After some time, he spoke with great difficulty saying, 'Bairns I doot yi'll hiv tae pit me home; me face is aal twisted; I think I must be takkan a shock.'

A ferrylouper new to Orkney and still not very familar with the geography of the islands got a job at what was then Baikie 's Woodyard in Kirkwall. Seeing a load of wood ready to go to the North Isles and marked *Miller, Papa Westray* he thought that couldn't be right so he corrected it. The new address read *Papa Miller, Westray*

Another story from the 'widyard'. But first of all the reader needs to be familiar with the Orkney dialect. In English 'cheap' and 'cheep' are pronounced identically. In the dialect of Orkney, this is not the case. Although 'cheep' is pronounced *cheep*, 'cheap' is pronounced *chaep*! The other piece of information the reader requires is that the word 'burded' in dialect applies to an egg which has a chicken inside. Now for the story.....One of the employees in the 'widyard' kept a few hens and on one occasion when he had a surplus of eggs he thought he would bring them in and sell them to his workmates. At 'piece time', he produced a box of eggs and announced, partly in dialect and partly in English, 'Wid yi like some eggs boys – thir gaan cheap.' 'Oh beuy,' said one, 'wir no gaan tae buy burded eggs.' 'Whit dae yi mean?' asked the vendor. 'Weel', his workmate replied, 'we'll mibbee buy eegs if thir gaan chaep, bit we'll no buy them if thir gaan cheep!'

The following story is a good illustration of the old saying 'Out of the mouths of babes.... etc'. On one occasion I was helping the infants to put on their winter coats while they waited for school transport. One little girl was having great difficulty putting on her coat and I went over to offer her help.

'What's the matter Hazel? (I'll call her).

'Hid's a terrible thing o coat this,' came the reply,'wan day me airm will go in the sleeve aal right bit hid generally goes doon the lining. Hid's no winder somebody pot hid tae Oxfam.'

This could also have been interpreted as 'Out of the mouths of babes........'

In the days before Parents' Meetings were held in schools, teachers would sometimes informally invite parents into classrooms to see what kind of work was being done. A Stromness parent was walking round the classroom with the teacher and her eye fell on an essay written by her daughter which was prominently displayed on the wall. A sentence in it read:-

> *My daddy is a baker and he has to get out of bed at 4 o'clock every morning. When he is gone, Joseph creeps into the bedroom and jumps in beside mother. She says he keeps her warm.*

The wife had a bit of explaining to do to the teacher. Although at that time they had a lodger called Joseph who was working on construction at the new pier, Joseph also happened to be the name of their dog.

An Orcadian who has a BT mobile 'phone took a call one evening.

'British Telecom, Janice speaking, is it a convenient moment to talk to you about some of the new services we offer?'

'Hid's no convenient at aal,' replied the man,'Ah'm in the middle o a lifeboat rescue' !

Many stories are told about a Harray wife who was something of a character and her son who was a bit of a tear-away. Most of these stories are apocryphal I am sure but it is the fate of such characters to have stories made up about them! When Maggie (we'll call her) learned from a neighbour that a young girl in the parish had become pregnant by her son she remarked calmly, 'Me peerie boy's gittan ferfil careless; hid wis only the tither day he brok a broom hanle.'

What a dramatic change of lifestyle a farmer must experience when he sells up and moves into a house in town. Some farmers hold on to their farm as long as they can, postponing the dreaded day. One such Birsay farmer rented out his land for many years while living in his farm-house. What a fine solution this was. Quite often in the summer time I would see him wandering through the fields, scythe in hand, cutting down the weeds. He must have been so happy that he was still able to do this. However the time came, as it must do inevitably, when he had to move into sheltered housing in Stromness. I went down to visit him.

'Weel hoo dae yi like hid here Eddie?' I asked.

'Oh, hid's aal right too in a wey Grigger beuy bit min thir's no a tirso aboot the place tae cut ava.'

Nowadays a farmer has a scientific instrument which can tell him the amount of moisture in a crop and whether it is advisable to combine. In the old days Orkney farmers were also able to tell the amount of moisture in a field and whether or not it was advisable to work in the harvest. They had no scientific instrument however. They used nature's own method. Before they went to bed at night they would urinate on a flag-stone at the end of the house and if the flagstone was dry in the morning they knew it would be a good day to harvest.

The following tale contains elements of both the above stories. A Graemsay farmer retired to a fine bungalow in Stromness in the 1950s. At the mart he met a fellow islander who asked whether he was happy about his move to Stromness.

'Hid's aal right too min in a wey,' came the reply, 'bit yi canna go tae the end o the hoose for a p....'

As we get older we are faced with a dilemma. Do we spend all our hard earned money or do we save as much of it as we can for emergen-cies or to pass on to our children? In his *Rubaiyat of Omar Khayyam* Edward Fitzgerald gave us this advice:

Ah, make the most of what we yet may spend
Before we too into the Dust descend.

An old Dounby philosopher, now gone, was in no doubt about what was the best course of action. 'Beuy,' he said,' settan doon his Smithfield pint, 'if yi die wi a pound in yir pooch hid's a pound waested. '

Many tales are told of dialect misunderstandings. We share with our Norwegian cousins the verb 'to ask' which in Norwegian is *spørre*. In Orkney it is usually written 'speer'. 'Yi'll hae tae speer the bung o the tar barrel', was an old retort to an impertinent question.

 It was a pouring night of rain when a hitch-hiker enquired at a house in Sandwick for bed and breakfast. The landlady said that she was sorry she was fully booked but if the visitor would like to jump in the car she would drive her to a neighbour who might be able to help. They arrived at the neighbour's house and the man of the house answered the door.

'I winder if thoo his a spare bed the night Ronnie for aal me beds are fill?' she asked.

'Oh lass Ah'll hae tae go an speer the wife,' came the reply and the man turned to go back in.

When he had gone the girl turned to her helper with a quizzical expression on her face, 'Did he say he was going to spear his wife?'

In the 1950s a Kirkwall firm sent a joiner out to Stronsay to put a new roof on a hennie-hoose for a owld wife.

'Whitiver yi deu beuy,' said the boss, 'don't come back withoot the money. That wife's a naafil bad payer. No money beuy and yi might be oot o a job.'

So the joiner went out to Stronsay with the North Isles boat, did the job and returned.

'I hop yi minded oan aboot the money,' the boss said.

'Oh yaas, hid's oot in the yaird.'

'Whit!' exclaimed the boss.

In the yard stood a tethered animal.

'The owld b★★★★★ widna gae me the money,' said the joiner, 'so I tuk her goat.'

After the first attack on Scapa Flow by enemy aircraft in World War II a Burray family feared for their lives and Sandy, the man o the hoose, thought it would be a good idea to build an air-raid shelter. Some further excavation of a small cave on the shore would make an ideal air-raid shelter he decided. He approached Willack, the neebor man, to see whether he would give him any help for both houses could easily share the cave in an emergency but Willack was normally not one to stir himself, especially where work was concerned.

'Ah, hid's aal right min, I widna git unduly concerned. Niver a bomb'll come near wir hooses.'

Sandy thought he would leave Willack to his fate and set into tackling the cave himself with pinch and mallet, pick and shovel, spending anxious days and nights on the back-breaking excavation. In the end he had built a fine retreat for his family with a few fish boxes scattered round for seats. The completion of the air-raid shelter was timely for shortly afterwards the air-raid siren went and all the family dashed down to the cave.

Sandy was speechless when he got there for sitting comfortably on a fish box at the far end was Willack.

'Ah'm just testan her,' he said!

Many of the tales told in Orkney are about the war since many of those who were young bloods at the time now have the leisure to recall some of the amusing happenings of that momentous period in the history of Orkney.

When Norway was invaded the whole political map of Europe, as far as Britain was concerned, was turned upside down with the realisation that invasion might come, not from the south, but from the north. Every thinking islander got caught up in the debate on the consequences for Orkney of such an event.

A South Ronaldsay man was not too perturbed about such a happening, 'They'll niver invade Orkney,' he affirmed, 'thir's far too much barbed wire'!

When several of the West Mainland schools were threatened with closure in the early '70s, Education Department officials convened a meeting in Sandwick to explain to parishioners that there was no future for the South Sandwick school; all pupils were to be transported to a purpose built school at Dounby. One parishioner was angered that the children had to get up so much earlier to meet the new school transport. He shook his fist at the officials on the stage.

'Hid's aal right for you lot up there,' he said, 'yi'll aal still be in yir beds when wir bairns are dirlan roond the perrish.'

How the world has shrunk! Frequently today, queries are handled by call centres in India. International routing of calls is not new. Eighteen years ago when Loganair was brought under the umbrella of British Regional Airways, timetabling queries were centralised to the main British Airways switchboard in Newcastle. When the Newcastle switchboard was overloaded all queries were automatically transferred to New York. An Orkney itinerant teacher who had been asked to go to Stronsay for a day rang Loganair in Kirkwall (as he thought) to check on the flight time. He was surprised to find that his query was answered by an operator in New York!

At the turn of last century Baikie's shop in Rendall, like all village shops, was well patronised. Mr Baikie himself was a popular figure and had all kinds of tricks up his sleeve for quick service. For instance if anyone ordered an ounce of 'black twist,' to smoke in his pipe Mr Baikie did not weigh it out but measured it from the tip of his finger to a little brown mark on his arm. No one ever queried this but one day a stranger came into the shop and ordered black twist. Mr Baikie 'weighed' it out in his customary manner.

'That's no right,' said the stranger, 'that's no a ounce.'

'Dae yi think no?' replied Mr Baikie.

He placed the tobacco on the weights, weighing it very accurately, then turning to the stranger he said, 'Yir fairly right min,' and taking out his knife he cut an inch off the end.

A fine (true) story is told by Alastair Marwick in his delightful book, 'Costa Heritage'. Alastair had heard the tale, passed down through the family, that one of his ancestors had courted a girl at Wasdale in Firth. To pursue the romance the relative had frequently walked from Costa to

Wasdale along the Birsay/Harray hill ridge, a distance of ten miles over rough terrain. Alastair decided one day to undertake this journey himself. When he came to the Lyde he met folk he knew who, not unnaturally, asked him what he was doing that day. Alastair replied that he was following in the footsteps of a man who had gone before him.

'My wir no seen him gan by', they said.

'That's no surprisan,' replied Alastair, 'he gid bye aboot a hunder and fifty 'ear ago'.

Hydro-Board engineers were called to a house in Dounby where the owner reported that he had no electricity and that there was something seriously wrong. The engineers found to their surprise that there had been something like an explosion round his meter. Asking the owner what had happened he replied that he had been demolishing an old building nearby and for safety sake he had turned off the electricity at the main. After the demolition of the old building was complete he turned the electricity on again and there was an almighty bang. 'What did you do with the wires going to the old building? ' he was asked. 'Weel', he replied, 'I tied them aal taegither tae stop the electricity escapan'!

A Stromness man became very hard of hearing in his old age and had particular difficulty on the telephone. His daughter-in-law had ordered turkeys for her family and for granny and telephoned to tell granny not to order her turkey for this had already been done. Unfortunately granny was out and grandad answered the telephone. The conversation was strained and difficult and went something like this:-

Daughter-in-law Tell Granny I ordered her turkey and it will be delivered on the 23rd....Turkey....TURKEY....It will be delivered on the 23rd...Tuesday...TUESDAY, the Tuesday before Christmas.

Grandad Tuesday?

Daughter-in-law Yes, Tuesday, that's right, it will be delivered on Tuesday (heaves a sigh of relief).

(A long pause follows)

Daughter-in-law Are you all right grandad?

Grandad Tell me wan thing lass. This thing yir spaekan aboot. Is hid animal, mineral or vegetable?

A favourite ploy of boys in the early years of last century was to play with gunpowder! In those days it was possible to buy saltpetre from the travelling van and gunpowder from a shop! Some boys at Huntscarth in Harray had made gunpowder and having made it, the next question was what to do with it. One suggested throwing it on the fire but there was some debate about whether this was safe or not. Eventually Bertie volunteered to throw it gingerly into the fireplace but they were a bit deflated when nothing happened.

'Blow on hid min,' shouted one.

Bertie duly puffed and blew. Suddenly there was an enormous flash and explosion which left him with no eyebrows and hardly any hair on one side of his head!

Such explosions must have been commonplace for the only reaction was a shout from great grandad out in the shed, 'Boys whit er yi deuan?'

Many years ago I had a letter from an elderly man in Australia who had gone to Stenness School before and during the 1st World War. He spoke of the boys' interest in explosives at that time:-

> Two schoolboys, Sidney Taylor and Alex Thomson (from Millhouse) got hold of a detonator used for blasting the roads. They set a match to it and it exploded and Alex who was about ten at the time had his right thumb halved. Sydney escaped with powder burns. It is lucky for them that the power of detonation goes down or they would have been much more severely injured. May Matches, then a 13 year old girl took both boys down to the schoolhouse for help. I remember the minister coming into the school and giving us all a pretty hot lecture and it was much needed for at that time gunpowder could be bought from any hardware shop. In fact at school a favourite trick used to be to fill empty 12 gauge cartridge cases with gunpowder and match heads and bang them between two stones. It would go off with quite a report! Of course the war (World War I) was on then and we got caught up in it in our own little way.

Clearly there was no playground supervision in those days! The old tradition of banging objects between stones was continued in my time as a teacher at Stenness but the activity did not have such an element of danger!

A favourite pastime of the boys was to find a flat stone, lay an unopened bag of crisps on it and giving it a good blow with another stone, flatten it and crunch the crisps to smithereens. I came across a group of boys doing this one day.

'What a stupid thing to do,' I said, 'do you realise that that firm pays out millions of pounds a year to make sure that you and all other children get nice, big, tattie crisps?'

They laughed.

I continued, 'I'm going to write to that firm and tell them not to bother packaging them safely for you just smash them up anyway.'

'Oh, don't do that sir,' an anguished chorus of voices said, 'for then we'll no hiv any fun!'

Bella had a nasty car accident not far from home when she accelerated instead of breaking on a corner and hit a concrete strainer with a terrific wallop. A neighbour was quickly on the scene. 'Are yi aal right Bella?' he asked, helping her out of the car.

'No so bad at aal,' she mumbled, 'bit I canna spaek very weel'.

The neighbour's first reaction was that she had had a stroke while driving but he soon realised what had happened. The force of the impact had caused Bella's false teeth to fly out of her mouth and they were lying on top of the dashboard!

And another story about false teeth! At the end of the war Stenness School had a very eccentric schoolmaster called Mr. Moar. One day Mr. Moar caught the bus to Kirkwall from what was then the old Post Office (now Sutherland's shop). The driver had gone as far as Barnhouse when he called out, 'Stop the bus – I've forgotten my teeth!'

Schoolmasters in those days always spoke 'proper', often in flowery language, no doubt to impress upon people that they were educated. On one occasion a parishioner asked Mr. Moar why he and his wife had no family. A sensible reply would have been, 'We couldn't have any children.' Mr. Moar replied in this way, 'We have ploughed and harrowed and we have sown but alas the seed has not germinated'!

Another instance of flowery language used by a headmaster was told me by one of my brothers. The usage was so ridiculous that even the children saw the funny side of it. It was the war time. Children were sitting quietly at their lessons in Firth School when there was a loud knock at the classroom door. The headmaster marched across the floor and all heads turned in anticipation of the sight of the stranger. There stood a dispatch rider in full gear.

'Are you Mr Tulloch?' he asked.

'I am he,' Mr. Tulloch replied!

Some old Orkney place-names are difficult to interpret. A good instance of this is the farm of Blowes in the Deerness. It was once occupied by a family by the name Aim. Were a family with such a name to live there today a Mart report might read, 'Forward at the Mart today were four heifers from Aim, Blowes, Deerness'! Six hundred years ago a man by the name Baddi lost all his land as a punishment for striking a man with such force in the Rendall kirkyard that he drew blood. He must have been a real baddy! Whether or not the man died we do not know. In the Deerness kirkyard is a tombstone which tells us that a man by the name Aim died, not of blows, but at Blowes!

A Stromness lady had a stroke and after hospital attention she was admitted to St. Peter's House. Her son worked in Brunei and she was anxious to write him a letter. However the stroke had affected her right arm badly and so she enlisted the help of one of the auxiliary staff to whom she dictated the letter.

Everything went well until it came to addressing the letter when there was some confusion over how BRUNEI should be spelt.

'Niver mind,' said the nursing assistant, 'Ah'll spell hid the wey I think hid should be spelt.'

The son in Brunei was astonished when he saw the address on the letter and even more astonished that the Post Office had been able to deliver it. The auxiliary must have thought that the old lady was speaking dialect for this was the address on the letter:-

Mr. Peter Sinclair (we'll call him)
Block 34
Tutonga
Bangar
Brown Eye

In the late 1930s, what was perhaps the most oddly addressed letter ever, was delivered by the the Eday postmaster. The sender was an a man by the name Swannie who was born at the Perk in Eday but who emigrated to USA and rose to became a Captain in the American Mercantile Marine. Like a number of Orcadians before him, he did not like his surname and after he had emigrated decided to adopt the name 'Swan'. Despite the change of domicile and surname he did not forget his native island and regularly communicated with local folk. He wrote a letter from America to the neebor wife in Breck in Eday telling her all his news. Imagine how she reacted when she saw how he had addressed it. The address read:

Postie when you're on the trot
Please take this to Mrs. Twatt
You'll find this dear and kindly lady
Amang the heather hills o Eday.

So devoted was Captain Jack Swan to the island of his birth that, before he died, he took the unusual step of having his gravestone erected, all suitably inscribed, to ensure that he would be buried on Eday. The only omission was the date of his death which the monumental mason arranged to be added at the appropriate time! Captain Jack's striking gravestone occupies a prominent position in Eday kirkyard and he would be thrilled to know that Orcadians still remember him.

In the 1960s a popular Shopping Week Review included a comic sketch based on the Robert Service poem *Dangerous Dan McGrew*. In the first performance the simple expedient of bursting a paper bag was used to represent the sound of Dan firing his gun. However the stage hand was completely dissatisfied with the result. He decided that for the next performance a louder explosion was warranted. Nothing less than a shotgun would suffice. A friend prepared the cartridge by removing the shot and the gun was furtively carried to the hall concealed in an old oilskin. At the critical moment in the play the trigger was pulled and such was the report in the close confines of the hall that the audience seemed to be lifted from their seats. But worst of all, during the firing, the wadding had ricocheted off the wall striking a member of the audience who put her hand to her chest and screamed. There was no doubt in the minds of the audience that she had been shot. But there was no blood, the audience settled down and the show went on.

The stage hand was delighted with his sound effect but when challenged later about the folly of discharging a shotgun in a small hall packed with people many of whom were small children he replied, 'Weel he wis <u>Dangerous</u> Dan McGrew efter aal.'

A Kirkwall lady who did bed and breakfast was busy with morning preparations for her American guests. While they were having cereal she turned on Radio Orkney for them and went out into the kitchen to cook breakfast. When she returned they were laughing their heads off. As one of them explained in deep Texan tones:-

'We've just been listening to your local radio station. The announcer said that they are scouring the countryside for someone who has no teeth for a set of false teeth has been found outside the Post Office. How could anyone lose their teeth? Must have been a violent sneeze or something! The landlady laughed with them and commented on the trifling little things that get mentioned on local radio.

When she returned to the kitchen she froze. Pondering for a moment she went outside to the hallway and checked the pocket of her coat. No they weren't there. The lost teeth were HERS! She had been to the dentist but the new teeth were so ill-fitting that she had taken them out, popped them in her pocket and put her old ones back in. They must have fallen out of her pocket as she got out of the car at the Post Office. When the landlady came in with the pot of tea, to her horror, the lost teeth were still the topic of conversation.

'We guess some guy's had too many Jack Daniel's, been sick and lost his teeth!' chortled the Texan.

It was too much for the landlady, 'Actually the teeth are mine,' she said boldly.

There was a stunned silence. But after an explanation the laughing started again. The Americans affirmed it was the highlight of their holiday!

When I was a teacher at Stenness School we talked about the advantages and disadvantages of living on an island. From there we moved to the subject of desert islands. 'Wouldn't it be fun to live on a desert island where you would be king or queen of the island and you could do what you want?' There was general agreement on this! I continued, 'Suppose that you could go and live on a desert island and you could choose to bring with you only one special thing, what would you bring? Write and tell me about that special thing'. Later on when I was correcting the pupils' essays I was intrigued by the choice made by one pupil, an English boy who had just recently joined the class. I spoke to him about his essay. 'You chose to bring your budgie Alex and you love him very much because he's so good at talking – and you would always have a companion. I like that very much – but why do you call him 'WASSO' – that sounds like an Orkney name'. 'No sir', came the confident reply, 'it's French'. 'It's French?' I asked him, quite puzzled. Then it suddenly dawned on me that Alex was right but I hadn't recognised the spelling. It should have been spelt OISEAU, French for 'bird'!

The farm of Upper Ellibister in Rendall was at one time owned by the Brass family. At the turn of the 20th century Mr Brass built a new barn with a fine blue Welsh slate roof. At Mr Brass's request the mason used a greenish coloured slate to mark out on the roof the initials WB for 'William Brass'. When the work was completed a neighbour called to inspect the work and eyed the initials on the roof.

'Whit does that letters stand for?' he asked Mr Brass.

Mr Brass obviously thought that such a stupid question deserved an equally stupid answer.

He tirled his kep on his head for a meenit and replied wi' a smile, 'Hid stands for WIR BARN'.

(by the way the initials can still be seen!)

A surveyor placed his theodolite in the courtyard of a farm in Harray. After a short while an old lady came out and surprised him by saying, 'Can I tak a luk through that?'

'If coorse,' he said obligingly, 'go ahead.'

She bent down and squinted through the lens. 'Mercy,' she said, 'everything's upside doon – I wid need tae tirl hid.'

'Yi better no deu that,' said the man, 'that thing cost thoosands o pounds!'

'Hid's funny yi should say that,' said the wife, 'for at the end o the war a man kam here like yirsael and pat a thing like that right in the middle o the yaird. And than he left hid and gid awey tae measure. Noo me brither niver saa this thing stanan in the yard and good he backid the cairt and horse right intae hid and dung hid doon and brok hid and the man wis most ferfil mad.'

They had a good laugh at that.

She studied the machine for a moment. 'Thoosands for that?' she queried, 'weel thank you anywey,' she said, 'thoo'll hiv tae get on wi thee wark and Ah'll hiv tae mak for in,' but as she turned towards the back door her foot caught in one of the tripod legs. The theodolite rocked violently and the shocked and anxious surveyor grabbed it and the old lady to steady them.

'Are yi aal right?' he asked.

She gave a little laugh, 'I nearaboot tirled hid efter aal,' she said.

Today when we buy a car we might think above all of reliability and safety features. This was apparently not so in the 1950s when a Harray man had two new cars in the space of three years at a time when it was fairly rare to have any sort of car, never mind a new car. He called at our family home one day to show off his new car.

The conversation with my brother went like this:-

'Whit dae yi think o hid Larrence?'

'My hid's no that long fae yi hid a new wan'.

'I ken, bit this wan's a piece better - far more CHRO<u>N</u>IUM on her.'

A devil-me-care Stromness farmer called at a garage in Finstown and said that he would like to buy a new car.

He was shown what the garage proprietor thought would be an ideal car for him. Opening the door he sat down in the driver's seat. He blew the horn.

'Ah, the horn wirks.'

Looking at the dashboard he exclaimed, 'My hid his a wireless!'

He turned it on and listened to the music for a while tapping his fingers on the steering wheel.

He turned off the radio, got out of the car, slammed the door and said to the astonished garage man, 'Right, Ah' ll hiv her. Hoo much?'

The attitude of MOT testing garages in the late 1960s left a lot to be desired. My first MOT test took place in Birmingham. The mechanic asked me to sit in the driving seat and turn on the lights. I obliged and he walked round the car.

'That's fine,' he said.

After kicking the front offside tyre, he took out his book and wrote the certificate!

In the 1980s a similar kind of thing must have happened in Orkney if the following story is true.

A man in his late 80s who had been a regular customer of the garage since well before the war always had his battered old car MOT tested at the same garage. The garage proprietor did not wish to offend the old man who rarely travelled more than two or three miles from home at little more than 20 mph and so he regularly wrote out a certificate but he always said to himself that he could not possibly pass the car another year.

One year Willie (we'll call him) came back for his annual test. When the car drove up to the garage with a clanking noise and with blue smoke pouring from the exhaust the garage proprietor turned away in despair. But then he had to face once more his most faithful customer.

'Ah'm comed for me test,' said Willie.

The garage proprietor thought for a minute. 'Beuy,' he says, 'if thoo goes tae the doctor and gets fae him a certificate for theesael tae say thoo're gan tae live anither 'ear, Ah'll pass thee car.'

'Whit wey dae I hiv tae deu that?' asked Willie in surprise.

'Becis,' the garage keeper went oan, 'if thoo dies the morn this car is gan tae be selt tae somebody else and hid's a bloody daeth trap.'

Kirkwallian Geordie Arthur was well known for his great knowledge of birds. Less well known was his interest in music. In fact he was an accomplished cello player; he played in the Kirkwall Orchestra and regularly attended practices. One evening he was walking up Bridge Street carrying his cello when he was hailed from across the street. 'Whar are thoo gaan Geordie beuy?'

'Awey tae play in the orchestra,' he answered.

'That's the stuff beuy, keep hid up min. Keep practisan and thoo'll soon be good enough for the Reel and Strathspey.'

Notice what the man said, 'Reel and Strathspey'. Normally one would say 'Strathspey and Reel' but Orcadians in daily speech have a habit of turning the content of phrases such as that back to front. There is no explanation for such behaviour. Here are some other examples:-

netting wire (wire netting), needles and preens (pins and needles), sole stockings (stocking soles), headlight (light headed), forks and knifes (knives and forks); ootside in (inside out). In the case of 'inside out', the English is much more logical for it is possible to see the inside when it's out but not the outside when it's in!

Then there is the strange Orcadian reversal in the sentence 'Yi suit hid' speaking of a jersey for example when English would normally say, 'It suits you'!

Have you ever had a jersey with a small different colour pattern in it, say a black jersey with a small red fleck in it? When such a jersey is 'fleeped', i.e. turned inside out, it is predominantly red. Now you can understand why a sooth country visitor was confused when looking at someone trying on a jersey and heard a friend say, 'Yi suit hid better when hid's ootside in.' In English this would be, 'It suits you better when it's inside out'!

A large Orkney lady, a farmer's daughter, could frequently be seen at the wheel of her father's tractor. Her hobby, strange to say, was dancing. She was well known for her love of dancing and her expertise on the dance floor and often appeared at dance halls in the West Mainland. On one occasion a small man took her up for an Old Time Waltz. He did not have the same skill on the dance floor as his partner and when it came to turning on the floor he could turn only clockwise. Round and round he went in the same direction until she almost became 'headlight'. The big lady tried to take control and turn him the other way but knowing that he would make a complete fool of himself he resisted this. Eventually in despair she called to him in a loud voice, 'Min can thoo no reverse?' She must have thought she was at the controls of her Fergie!

I have spoken about my granny before. You will remember that I described her as a tough old character. One moonlight night she had to go a message and her path took her past the lonely Rendall kirkyard. Everything went well on the outward journey but on the return she was just passing the kirkyard wall when two ghostly figures appeared above the wall wailing in lugubrious tones 'W-e h-a-v-e r-i-s-e-n f-r-o-m t-h-e d-e-a-d.' At this point most sensible people would have taken to their heels. But not granny. She stopped in her tracks and had a good look at them.

'Oh,' she says, 'whit's yir message?'

The figures slipped below the wall again.

As granny walked on she heard one say to the other, 'Yi'll no frighten that owld b★★★★★.'

My grandad had been to the market and had bought for himself a pair of trousers. Of course he had no opportunity to try them on until he came home. He was very proud of his purchase and immediately went into the bedroom to change. Emerging with his new trousers on he turned round on the floor to show them off. They were clearly very ill fitting.

'Whit dae yi think o them Hughina?' he said to granny.

Granny snorted disdainfully, 'Huh,' she said, 'yi wid need a bow o mael tae fill the erse o them.'

One night an elderly Finstown lady went for her customary short walk in the grimlings. When she returned she was very pale and out of breath and slumped down on a chair.

'Whit's the metter granny?' they asked.

'Ah'm gotten a terrible fright,' she said. 'I wis walkan up by Kelday's butcher shop when a great big buss o heather kam flyan doon the road on hid's own at a ferfil speed and nearaboot dung me doon.'

The family immediately thought that granny had walked too energetically and had begun to hallucinate or that she had begun to dote. They cross-examined her about what she had actually seen and she was adamant that it was a buss of heather travelling under its own steam down the road.

After some time the family learned that Granny had become the victim of the village prankster – a man in his forties who never wanted to grow up. On this occasion, much to the amusement of the young lads outside the Pomona Inn, he had fixed to his bicycle a very long black string to the end of which he had tied a huge bunch of heather. He had set off downhill with the bunch of heather travelling more than a hundred yards behind him. When granny was told the true story she said, 'I ken fine yi thowt I wis dotan bit noo yi'll mibbe listen tae me.'

The fine old Orkney expression 'weel amis' means 'well deserved'. Let me give the reader an illustration of how it is used. One summer evening in the 1960s I was looking for the house of Fursebreck in Harray. Not having much success I knocked on the door of a small cottage. I heard a voice call, 'Come in!' I couldn't believe what I heard. It would be very unusual even in easy going Orkney at that time to be immediately invited in after knocking on a door. I knocked once more and I heard the same voice call, 'Come in,' so in I went.

There was an old lady sitting beside the fire knitting who looked absolutely astonished when I came into her living room.

'My, whar are thoo?' she gasped.

I explained my simple mission.

'Mercy me, I thowt hid wis Jean fae next door.' She roared and laughed in her embarrassment, 'Hid wis weel amis,' she said.

Here is another instance of the use of that expression. I have to admit that my pranks have <u>usually</u> been in good taste. On one occasion as a headteacher I played a prank on a parent – rather a dangerous thing to do but I think that by this time I have been forgiven.

The mother of a boy spoke to me about her son and how badly behaved he was at home. 'Whit's he like in school?' she asked.

I was able to assure her that her son Peter (we'll call him) was no trouble at all. In fact I really liked him and we got on well together. She found my remarks unconvincing and went on, 'I dreed the day that you appear on me doorstep wi him.'

A short while later the school tape recorder broke down and I needed one urgently. Peter put up his hand, obliging boy that I always found him to be, 'Please sir,' he said, 'Ah'll lend yi mine.'

'That's very good of you Peter,' I said, 'I'll take you up on that if you think your mother would let me borrow it.'

Accordingly, at lunch time Peter and I jumped in the car and we set off for his house.

On the way there, his mother's fear that I would sometime appear on her doorstep with him flashed through my mind. The opportunity for a good trick became apparent.

Turning to Peter I said, 'When yir mither sees iss both arrive I baet she thinks hid's becis yir done something terrible in school. I want yi tae behave as if yir done something terrible. Hing yir head doon when I knock on the door and just listen tae whit I say.'

Mother appeared and her face dropped when she saw us. 'Ah'm come aboot your son Peter,' I said with a sober face.

'Oh whit's he done noo?' she asked frowning at him.

'Oh nothing,' I said, 'I wid just like tae borrow his tape recorder.'

She fixed me with a steely glare, 'You b-gg-r o hell!' she said and vanished inside.

Peter fetched his tape recorder and we drove back to school. After a short while Peter broke the silence, 'I think yir joke kinda misfired,' he said!

I must be the only headmaster to have had the dubious honour of being addressed in such a manner by a parent but, as they say, 'Hid wis weel amis!'

Two Rousay tradesmen worked next door to each other in a small building. The one end was occupied by a blacksmith and the other by a joiner. There was a hole in the wall which divided the two properties by which both tradesman benefited; sometimes the long lengths of metal used in the smithy could be worked properly only if they could be shoved through the hole and similarly long battens were pushed through from the joiner's shop on the days when he was sawing. So, between them, there was quite a bit of cooperation but all that came to an end as a result of a trick which one played on the other.

One day the blacksmith got word that the minister was coming to see him and this upset him because he couldn't be bothered with him. When he saw the reverend make his way to the workshop he dashed into the joiner's shop and asked the joiner where he could hide.

'Ap there min on the planks on the twartbacks,' said the joiner - and that's where the blacksmith took refuge.

The minister banged on the door of the blacksmith's for a bit then he came to the door of the joiner's shop.

'Excuse me,' he said, 'you haven't seen the blacksmith anywhere, have you?'

'Oh yaas, he's ap there,' replied the joiner, pointing to the blacksmith crouching up above him!

The next day the blacksmith bricked up the hole in the wall and from that day on the families never spoke.

A former Cathedral minister told of an embarrassing incident in his early days as a minister in Glasgow. He was visiting a family in a tenement block and being a first visit, he was keen to make a good impression. He was interested to find on his arrival that the family had a budgie which made a good opportunity to open a conversation. The family was very proud of the budgie and for the minister's benefit, opened the cage and let it fly round the room. The minister meanwhile took up a position by a roaring coal fire awaiting a cup of tea while he talked to the 'man o the hoose'. All the while the budgie was flying round the room swooping and diving. On one of these passages it swooped down in front of the minister but unfortunately just as at that moment the minister crossed his legs, hitting the budgie with his shoe and kicking it into the blazing fire!

When I was a pupil at Stromness Academy I spent a summer holiday as a porter at the Stromness Hotel. One day I was asked to come down to reception because there was a young French girl there who had some kind of problem and no one could understand what she was saying.

Here was my first opportunity to speak French to a real French person. When I arrived at reception there were two girls there - both about the same age. One immediately began to tell me what the problem was. She had lost her purse somewhere in Stromness; she had been in the hotel. Had anyone in the hotel found the purse? When I explained this to the receptionist she replied that no purse had been handed in. I translated this to the French girl who shrugged her shoulders and turned to go. I was so flushed with my success in acting as interpreter that I turned to whom

I assumed was the girl's friend and enquired, 'Vous êtes française, vous aussi?'

'Oh, no' she replied, 'jist plain Aiberdeen.' She had just come for a job interview!

Age doesn't make us any more sensible. In Milan recently I looked forward to practising my Italian which I had been learning for more than a year. I knew I was on the correct platform at the station and I knew exactly when the train was arriving, 'but', I said to myself, 'why don't I go over to that smartly dressed, swarthy looking gentleman over there and engage him in conversation.'Is this the correct platform for Seregno?' I asked in impeccable Italian. He looked at me with a puzzled expression.'Do you speak English?' he asked.'Yes,' I replied, disappointed.'Well,' he said, 'shall we speak in that language then because I'm Pakistani'.

A British ambassador in a foreign country sent a strongly worded memo to the Foreign Office in a desperate attempt to be awarded more funds so that he could employ more staff. To stress the need for this he said that on the last occasion the Foreign Secretary had visited the country for which he was responsible the Foreign Secretary himself had stayed at the Embassy and at night had left his shoes outside the door to be cleaned. They could not afford to keep a night porter and the ambassador's wife had to clean the Foreign Secretary's shoes herself!

This brings to mind another incident when I was a porter at the Stromness Hotel. Jim, another boy out of my class, was the night porter. We both lived in, staying in attic rooms at the top of the hotel.

I frequently used to go down in the late evenings and have a chat with Jim since being a night porter was a pretty lonely job. One of Jim's jobs was to go round the corridors at night collecting shoes, putting the room number on them of course, that was important, cleaning them thoroughly and returning them. I sometimes helped him.

One night we were sitting talking. Jim was cleaning shoes as usual. As we talked he said, 'Some of the folk that come here hiv terrible shoes Grigger – just luk at this pair.'

I looked at them in disbelief. Sure enough the brown leather was cracked and there was a big hole in the sole of one of them.

We wondered why people who were rich enough to live in the hotel couldn't afford a decent pair of shoes.

Well Jim, after all these years I can now make a confession. I was going to a dance in Stromness that night and looking at my shoes I thought they were in such a terrible state that they needed some work done on them so I put them outside Room 10.

Yi made a good job o them Jim beuy!

Many years ago we were driving through Bulgaria on our way to Turkey. I thought it would be a shame not to see the famous Valley of the Roses and so we made a little detour to Stara Zagora. Unfortunately the signposting in Bulgaria at that time was not very good and to make matters worse the writing was in the Cyrillic script so it wasn't a case of simply reading the roadsigns as we went along. We had to stop and work out what each one meant.

This became a little tedious and so after some time I felt I needed some reassurance that we were travelling in the right direction. Seeing an old man sitting on a grassy bank at the edge of the road I stopped the car and went over to him. I pointed ahead and said 'Stara Zagora.' He shook his head but at the same time he smiled. This confused me so I asked him again. I got an identical reaction which seemed to suggest that he knew where Star Zagora was but he wasn't going to tell me. I gave up and went back to the car.

'Are we on the correct road?' asked Elizabeth.

'I have no idea,' I replied, 'it was a completely stupid person I asked – he sat there grinning and shaking his head.

However as we travelled on I just happened to remember what I had read in a guide book. In certain parts of Bulgaria the word 'No' is accompanied by a nodding of the head but a 'Yes' is accompanied by a shaking of the head – exactly the opposite of everywhere else! In our culture it is extremely difficult to shake one's head, smile and at the same time say 'Yes'. Try it! It was comforting to realise that we were on the right road after all.

An old Orkney folk tale speaks of the 'Maister Ship', a gigantic vessel which had formerly plied the seas. Here is the same tale told with some literary licence . . .

When the American space team landed on the moon in 1969, they were surprised to find in the area known as *Mare Tranquilitatis* an old man sitting on a rock and beside him, lodged in the moon dust, a yellow flag which had in the Scandinavian fashion a horizontally displaced red cross. Now the truth can be told. The first man to set foot on the moon was not Neil Armstrong from Wapakoneta in Ohio but Willie John Bress from Windywalls in Firth. It's a long story.

At one time the largest sailing ship which sailed the world's oceans belonged to an Orcadian. No description of the vessel would convey adequately its size but the tale is told of a violent Atlantic storm which she weathered, a tale in which we learn that the gigantic Korean shipyards of today are but Lilliputian Legoland constructions compared with the dock in which the so called Maister Ship was born.

In the violent storm I speak of, Willie John Bress, at that time a swack young man, was ordered by the bo'sun to climb aloft and reef the topsail. He reached the top only with great difficulty, his leg muscles showing all the symptoms of old age for by the time he gained the mast-top he was 82 years old. He had just begun to furl the topsail when the Maister Ship was thrown into the air by a towering wave more than 1000 feet high. By the greatest misfortune it was just passing the moon at that time and though the ship had been designed in such a way that the masts would always clear any heavenly bodies the top of the mast struck the moon a violent blow. Willie John held on tightly but there was no strength left in his arms and he was thrown clear. He grabbed a flag fluttering at the mast head in a desperate bid to regain his grip but it was no use – the flag came away and Willie John was thrown on to the moon's surface. What could he do now? He stuck the flag deep into the dust, sat on a rock and waited and waited, looking down on Windywalls in the far distance. He waited for 1000 years. Suddenly to his astonishment he saw one day a spacecraft slowly float down to the surface.

Out stepped one man then another. Willie John tried to get up to greet them but he could not move. His knees had locked. They came over to him.

'Say buddy, are you all right?' asked Neil Armstrong.

The shock was too much for Willie John. He keeled over and died.

But Willie John has not been forgotten. To this day part of the moon's surface is called *Mare Tranquilitatis Windywallis*.

Weel bairns, that's me story. When owld folk spoke aboot the man in the moon they wir fairly right. Bit I baet yi didna ken hid wis Willie John Bress o Windywalls.

As a student I went hitch-hiking with another classmate to Switzerland. When we reached London we found that it was practically impossible to get hostel accommodation. Our only hope we were told was a private hostel at the Elephant and Castle. We set off in the direction suggested but after some time sought reassurance from a policeman.

'Could you tell us where the Elephant and Castle is?' I asked.

He looked the two bedraggled figures up and down.

'Why do you want to go there mate?' he asked, 'ain't no castle there and ain't no elephant nyver.'

But after the joke he was most helpful. We certainly had better luck than the Harray man who lost his way in London before the war. He stopped a passer-by with the reasonable request, 'Can you tell me the way to Euston Station?'

The man proceeded to walk on and snapped over his shoulder, 'Do you know the population of London mate?'

A bit surprised the Orcadian blurted, 'About nine million,' I think.

'Yeah, nine million,' he shouted, now at some distance, 'so why the bloody hell ask me?'

Robert Rendall, the Orkney poet, was a real gentleman I'm told. He was also very fond of Italy and visited that beautiful country whenever he could. He told this story to a friend.

He was travelling in a railway carriage in Italy and was joined in the compartment by a dignified Italian lady carrying a handbag and a small knapsack. He knew a little Italian and they were able to exchange a few pleasantries.

After a short while the lady opened the knapsack on her knee. It was her lunch pack and she offered Robert to partake but Robert, being a gentleman, declined. He sat looking out of the window while the lady enjoyed her lunch. When she had finished, the kerchief lay on her knee covered with crumbs. Robert chivalrously rose from his seat, carefully lifted the four corners of the kerchief containing the crumbs, opened the window and shook the kerchief outside. Unfortunately the wind carried away the kerchief too!

An old Rendall man who frequently told tall stories was boasting about his expertise with a shotgun when he was young.

'I was doon at the Loch o Isbister wan night wi the gun when a great flock o wild geese kam ower. I lifted me gun beuy and let fly at them and if I tuk doon wan I must hiv taen doon a dizzen.'

The incredulous listener said, 'Hid's impossible min tae kill a dizzen wild geese wi wan shot.'

'Oh no,' the old man went on, 'the secret is this. Just when yi pull the trigger yi shack the barrel at the same time. Spreads the shot yi see.'

In the old days Orkney men often indulged in trials of strength; it must have been something to do with their Norse background. Here is a typical show of prowess. A miller in Stenness used to be able to lift a fully grown man on a mill shovel till his head touched the ceiling! He could also write his name on the wall with a 56lb. weight on his winkie!

Many tales were told of such men. Of course it gave the storyteller plenty of opportunity for exaggeration. One man describing an old fellow in his heyday who could not be matched for strength said of him, 'He hid a most ferfil grip in his hand min. He wis the only fulloo I ever kent that could hurl a burroo load o dung and wave tae yi at the sam time.'

A Westray couple had a son who was stationed near Gloucester during the war and who used to write to his parents regularly. On one occasion the letter they received from him had a portion missing; it had clearly been cut out by the censor. They were intrigued by this and when he came home on leave they showed him the letter and asked if he remembered what he had written. He remembered it well. It was not very far away from his camp where the jet aircraft was being developed and he had seen the prototype fly quite frequently. He had described the sound of the aircraft as it passed overhead. As he explained to his parents:–

Aal I wrote wis 'a new kind of plane is being developed down here. It makes a completely different sound. It reminds me of an iron wheeled barrow going over flagstones.'

It was a pretty good description of the sound. The censor must have been an Orcadian!

Some ten years ago I met a man who had been an officer in the Royal Navy based at Hatston during World War II. For a short period one of his duties had been to act as a censor. One day he opened a letter to find that the writer was no other than Yehudi Menuhin who at that time was touring Orkney. In the letter the young Yehudi gave a good description of his movements in Scapa Flow – which also happened to give a good description of the disposition of Fleet! The censor had no choice but to resort to the scissors! I later had some correspondence with Yehudi Menuhin who could not remember writing the letter but who vividly recalled his stay in Orkney.

I was at Baikie's shop in Finstown some twenty years ago. In the shop doorway I met a well known Finstown man, a friend of the family, whom I hadn't seen for many years. After a few exchanges I asked him, 'Whar are yi wirkan noo Robbie (we'll call him).'

'Oh, still wi the County Council, I doot Grigger, Ah'll be there till the end o me days.'

'Whar's thee brither wirkan noo?' he asked.

'Oh he's in Persia,' I replied.

'In Persia, goodness me,' he said. Robbie was a bit of a wag. I could see him thinking. He went on,' He'll be wi the Persian County Council likely.'

In the old days library books were delivered to schools in a wooden box and they were returned at the end of term. At Firth School it was the custom for some of the senior pupils to fill the box at the end of term and carry it to the school door ready for collection. A wooden box full of library books can be extremely heavy and on one occasion it was so heavy that the headmaster himself could not lift it. The pupils had devised a clever trick. Spurred on by workmen at the school, one of whom had been a former pupil, they borrowed from them at playtime a hammer and nails and nailed the box to the floor. When it came to carrying the box to the door, the pupils said to the headmaster that it was so full of books that they could not lift it.

'Out of my way, weaklings!' said the headmaster and grasping the box firmly attempted to lift it but it would not move. He strained again with no success. When a pupil burst out laughing, the game was up!

When I was a primary school pupil in Firth there was a boy there a bit older than myself called Benjie, an able boy and extremely witty. One of his specialities was to explain the significance of the letters of car number plates. Here are two examples of his wit that I can recall. At that time only two cars came to the school every day. One car, a black Austin, transported pupils to and from School. It was driven by Andrew Baikie and the registration letters were ASC. Benjie said that this stood for ALL SCHOOL CHILDREN. The other car, a little dark red Morris delivered milk from Grandon dairy. The registration letters of this car were DSM. No problem for Benjie. It stood for DIRTY SOOR MILK. I hope Grandon will forgive me for Benjie's interpretation – it was fifty years ago after all. Personally I can recall the lovely creamy milk which Grandon always supplied!

I was on playground duty in a Birmingham secondary school and my attention was drawn to a little group of boys in a far corner cheering. When I approached them I saw a little first year Irish boy lying on the ground.

'What's up?' I asked, forcing my way through the cordon of spectators.

'It's all right sir, it's only Kevin; he'll be OK in a minute.'

'What do you mean it's only Kevin?' I asked.

'It's Kevin trying to make some pocket money.'

'What do you mean? What's going on?' I insisted. I bent down to look at him. To me he seemed to be dead.

Then the story unfolded. Kevin regularly performed a trick for pupils but only if he collected enough sixpences from the spectators. With several sixpences in his pocket he would squat down for some time with his head between his legs like the little showman he was. Then he would shoot quickly up into the air. This quick movement affected the blood supply to his brain and he would collapse in a dead faint taking some time to recover! Kevin recovered sure enough and sat up smiling.

'Did ye see me surr?' he asked.

What could I say? He showed considerable enterprise even if it was rather risky. Today he is probably a successful Birmingham businessman.

In a review of my *Orkney Wordbook*, a dictionary of the dialect of Orkney, a German professor and expert on the dialects of English criticised me for including the word 'vanman'. He felt that it is so English and has such an obvious meaning (a man driving a van) that it should not have been included. How wrong he was. 'Vanman' had a very specific meaning in Orkney – the regular driver of one of the large mobile <u>grocery</u> vans which were so common at one time and such an important part of the rural scene. He not only sold goods, he would barter, post letters, deliver the odd parcel and most important of all, pass on the local news. To say 'the vanman telt me' was to give a piece of news the stamp of authenticity. And the vanman had long hours; we marvel today at the fact that city shops are open so late but in Orkney it was not unusual to meet 'the van' at 11 o' clock at night! The demise of the Orkney grocery van must have been a heartfelt blow to the Orkney countrywoman. It inspired me to write the well known dialect poem *Mary Annie Flett*.

In the early days, 'the van' was drawn by a horse and one of the longest runs was on the island of Sanday. When he had served his last customer at the North End, the vanman would point his horse in the homeward direction and, exhausted, go to sleep. Late one night some mischievous boys seeing the horse van come along and the driver asleep took hold of the reins and keeping it walking, turned it right round in the road and sent it back in the direction it came. The reaction of the vanman when he awoke back once more at his last customer does not need to be described!

It is difficult to believe that before the war a vanman was the victim of a highway robbery, perhaps the only instance of this offence that has ever occurred in Orkney. Fortunately no violence occurred. When Isbister's van returned to Quoyloo after a typically long day the driver, fortunately in this case also the shop owner, found that his money box was missing. As can be imagined there was quite a lot of money in a vanman's box at the end of a day which must have been a great temptation to anyone. But how had the thief got away with it? There was only one possible explanation. There was very little power in the engine of the pre-war vans and on the return journey from Stromness it had to negotiate a hill at walking pace. At this point the thief must have quietly jumped on the van and removed the till. With the noise of the engine the driver would have had no hope of hearing any movement behind him. Whoever Orkney's 'Dick Turpin' was, he was never discovered.

Everyone knows that there is a high concentration of folk with the surname Flett in Harray. The story is told that at one time the Harray football team was made up of ten Fletts and one Johnston. When an observer asked why it wasn't possible to have eleven Fletts the secretary replied that, try as they might, they 'couldna find a left-feeted Flett'!

At Stenness Primary school, a highlight of the school year for the senior pupils was our annual cycling expedition. This started in a modest way cycling to the Ring o Brogar, to Harray, to Orphir and so on. The further we went, the more confidence we gained. Eventually we crossed the Pentland Firth with the St. Ola taking our bikes with us. At that time we could also take our bikes on the train free and so more than once we were able to cycle in the wilds of Ross and Cromarty.

One year I arranged the cycling expedition as usual and arrangements were well in hand when a pupil came to the desk one day and said, 'Mr. Lamb, I hop yir mindan on thit I canna go a bike.'

My jaw must have dropped three inches. I had completely forgotten about the pupil who had never ridden a bike. My first reaction was to abandon the whole scheme for I could not possibly leave one pupil behind.

As I drove home that night I had an idea. Maybe he could not ride a bike but could he ride a tandem? Could anyone who had never ridden a bike ride a tandem? If he could ride a tandem he could come after all. I had a friend Tony who had an old tandem. Perhaps he could answer that question and, more important would he allow me to borrow it, I wonder? I went to see him. Yes he thought it was possible for anyone who had never ridden a bike to ride a tandem. Then he asked me how much experience I had on a tandem. I had to confess I had never been on one! But he was a good sport and invited me to take the tandem down to school to see how things went. The various experiments in the school playground were a great success; both the pupil and I were very confident that we could manage.

The expedition went ahead. When we came off the St. Ola the first challenge lay ahead - cycling to the Railway Station in Thurso. Now I need not remind the reader that just outside Scrabster is a very steep hill which we launched into at full speed. But half way up I ran out of gears and jumped off in a great hurry temporarily thinking I was on a bicycle with the result that the first my tandem partner knew of my decision was a terrible smack on the side of his head when my foot hit him! Shocked and dazed he said, 'Yi didna tell me yi wir stoppan.' Ever after that he was always off the bike first or at least ducked as the boom of my leg swung over him!

I developed a good working relationship with my tandem partner. We were able to cycle up some very steep hills in Ross-shire and to experience the sheer joy of whooshan down the other side at about 30 mph! On this old bone-shaking tandem the rushing air sometimes gave me the feeling of being the wartime pilot of a Swordfish bi-plane as I called to my navigator behind. On one occasion rushing madly downhill I shouted to him over my shoulder, 'Open your mouth wide and you'll catch some flies.'

'I canna do that sir', came the reply, 'Ah'm a vegetarian'!

A Birsay man and his wife had been visiting folk at the Sooth End in Stromness. When they were there a lady from the North End happened to visit too. They all had a pleasant afternoon together and when it came to going home the Birsay man offered the lady from the North End a lift which she accepted. His wife and the Stromness lady jumped into the back of the car to finish their yarning and the car set off. He stopped at the North End, let the lady out, called 'Cheerio' and drove off. Arriving back in Birsay he pulled up in front of the garage and waited for the wife to open the door for him. But he waited..... and waited. Turning round, there was no wife to be seen! He quickly reversed out and drove back to Stromness as fast as his old Hillman would go. He was relieved to see his wife standing at the North End even if she was jumping mad! When the Stromness lady had got out of the car his wife thought that she would jump out too and go in the front seat. The only trouble was that she did not make this clear to her man who drove away and left her on the pavement!

The life cycle of man and woman is like the life cycle of a volcano. When young they are fiery and explosive and when old just a 'pair o owld craturs', so went the caption of an old cartoon in a Scottish newspaper I read in the 50s.

When we are young it is very difficult to imagine the fiery, explosive nature which characterised the youth of the elderly person with whom we come in contact. As we get older ourselves this becomes much easier. At one time for instance if I were confronted by a slow doddery driver on the road I might have muttered a few curses under my breath. Now I temper such emotions by believing that the driver in front was a war-time fighter pilot.

When I was very young we had lovely neighbours, a shepherd, Jimmy Henderson and his wife Jessie. To me at that time Jessie seemed very, very old. One day she told me (I would have been about seven years old at that time) that when she was a young girl she went with a friend to a concert in a village hall in Caithness where she was living at that time. They had a good trick up their sleeves. They arrived early bringing with them a little paper bag full of pepper and as they walked up the centre of the hall to their seats they sprinkled pepper in the corridor. As people came into the concert they stirred up the pepper dust and before long everyone in the hall was sneezing violently, including themselves. They practically ruined the concert but the culprits were never found out! I remember thinking how difficult it was for me to imagine 'old' Mrs Henderson behaving like that!

Some time afterwards when Jessie and Jimmy were out my sister and I took advantage of the opportunity to hop over the garden wall and have a bean feast – or rather a pea feast – of Jessie's lovely garden peas. However we had stupidly left the shells behind as evidence. Soon after her return home Jessie appeared angrily at the door with a handful of pea shells.

'Yir the culprits, I ken yi are!' she ranted at the door as we held on to mother's peenie. Our mother was mortified to learn that we had done such a thing. I only wish I had the sense then to remind Jessie about the tricks she had got up to when she was young!

Another lovely old lady called Ellen Tulloch lived not far away down at Binscarth Farm. She was the dairymaid – the traditional dairymaid who milked the cows as well as making cream, butter and cheese. We could stand at a distance and watch her milking but if we annoyed her she would give us a squirt of milk in the face. Of course it was fun to get a squirt of warm milk in the face and so we played up often getting thrown out of the byre in the end. Talking of milk reminds me that, at the time I speak of, Ellen called me 'Teethless Tammy' for it was at that time in our early lives when all our milk teeth melt away!

Ellen was a wonderful baker and baked regularly on Thursdays. Her speciality was shortbread and for some strange reason my sister and I always appeared at her doors on Thursday afternoons. We were invariably rewarded with a large piece of shortbread. One Thursday afternoon we went down to the farm as usual; Ellen 's door was open; we called. No reply. We peeped in. No Ellen – but a huge pile of freshly baked shortbread on a tray at the end of the table and that wonderful, warm, homely smell of new baking. No Ellen meant no shortbread for us but we weren't going to be outdone. We quickly dashed into her kitchen, grabbed a piece of shortbread each and ran outside. We looked round and could see no one. But haven stolen the shortbread, could we eat it? No! We had a huge twinge of conscience. It would be a mean trick to eat Ellen's shortbread; we would hide it. Straight across from Ellen 's was the cart shed with two or three carts in place. We ran in, climbed up on the carts and concealed the shortbread pieces on top of the cart shed couples. And they could be there yet for all I know. We certainly never ate them.

Many years later when I was at university I went down to see Ellen then in her eighties and still her usual cheery self. We swopped many yarns about earlier days and I felt humbled when she said, 'My I did enjoy you bairns coman aboot.' But even at the mature age of twenty I still couldn't bring myself to tell her about the day we stole her shortbread!

There is an old Russian folk tale about a man who told people that he could make soup from a stone. When I read this story to children once it reminded me of an Orkney story of soup made from harrow teeth! The story is set at Binscarth Farm.

Binscarth Farm was one of the few Orkney farms which had a 'bothy'. It was a large attic room above the hay shed and little piggery where, before the war, temporary workers lived and fended for themselves for there was a large open fire with a cruik on which they could cook. As a child I knew the bothy only as a large storeroom where a few sacks of grain were stored. When the door was opened mice could be seen dashing in every direction and we would scurry around to try and catch them. I did succeed in doing this on one occasion, only to get a nasty bite in the finger which ended that game.

I am told that before the war 'Jock' was one of the extra farm workers who appeared every harvest and took up residence in the bothy. When it came to fending for himself he would go out into the farmyard, grab a hen, thraa its neck and make soup about it. This came to the ears of Robert Scarth, the owner of Binscarth, who did not see frequent free hens as part of the contractual agreement. One night, presumably after a tip-off, he made a swoop on the bothy to find Jock sitting at the open fire stirring a big pot of soup. After a few words about the harvest and Jock's comfort he asked Jock what he had in the pot. Jock thought for a moment then holding up the old harrow tooth with which he was stirring the pot he said, 'Ah'm makkan harrow teeth soup.' Mr. Scarth laughed and after that witty remark could not bring himself to raise the question of the disappearing hens. As for Jock he must have realised that he had had a narrow escape for after that there was no further depletion of the flock of Binscarth fowls!

At the beginning of the Second World War Scapa Flow was strafed by several waves of German bombers. One bonny moonlight night in Orphir Peter walked down the road a piece to see his neebor Alfie. They had a long yarn mostly about the war and the changes that were occurring in the islands. When it came to supper time Alfie set the table with some plain fare and put two eggs in a pan on the stove to boil. The conversation continued but was soon brought short by the drone of German bombers approaching. 'Git under the table beuy!' Alfie shouted. The droning became louder and louder and soon they could hear the muffled sound of exploding bombs. Suddenly all hell was let loose as the guns of the Scapa defences opened up. The very walls of the house shook and two loud explosions sent shells flying through the kitchen. 'Wir been hit beuy', said Peter, 'thir's pieces o yir ceiling fallan doon.' 'Are yi aal right beuy, Alfie?' 'Ah'm fine min'. The gunfire continued for some time and when they heard the all clear sound from the ships in the Flow they crept out from under the table. 'My thir's something burnan,' said Peter. 'Hid is indeed', remarked Alfie. There was black smoke coming from the stove.

They soon realised that they hadn't been hit at all. True, shells had been flying round the room – but they had been egg shells. In the excitement of the attack, the boiling eggs had been forgotten about. The pan had boiled dry and the eggs had exploded!

When we hear of Orkney folks dashing off to USA or Australia – even Japan, for their annual holiday we should stop and think about the dramatic transformation that has overcome our lives in the last twenty years. Here is a story to illustrate this.

Grew in Birsay lies on the hill slope just above the 'new' Birsay kirkyard on the links in that part of the parish known as the Soothside or Birsay-Besooth. Murray Paterson of Grew told me that when he was a young man before the first World War his father told him to go to The Hass with a load of hay where his father had made a bartering arrangement. Bartering was common in those days; in this case a load of hay was to be bartered for a load of peats. The house called The Hass is one of the most isolated in Birsay right up on the side of the hill above Dirkadale. While he was unloading the hay a very old lady came out and spoke to him asking him where he came from. When he told her, she astonished him by saying that though she had been to Marwick she had never been to the Soothside – at most only five miles away!

This story has to be seen in context however. It would be wrong to think that Orcadians did not travel very far in those days. On the contrary there were those who went to the ends of the earth. Peter Hunter of Skorne in Marwick captained a vessel which took settlers to what is now the centre of Melborne. The folk of Melborne not only remember him; they built a replica of his ship which can be seen in the harbour there.

Firth School lies right at the edge of the sea but at that point the Bay of Firth is very shallow and normally there is no danger to the children from its position. However during the war when I was an infant pupil there was an exceptionally high tide when the sea came right over the approach road to the school. In those days there was no playground supervision and many pupils found the sight of the encroaching sea very exciting. We were all wading around in it. Unfortunately one infant pupil waded out too far, fell over the low defensive wall right into the sea and disappeared. He came up again screaming. There were gasps from us all but one of the big boys jumped in and pulled him out. I remember this incident vividly for two reasons. The boy was one of several English pupils who had recently come to school, his father being a serviceman stationed in Orkney. He had a most unusual name which he always reeled off in full when he was asked. At a time when schools were filled with boys with ordinary names like William Clouston or John Donaldson he was styled Richard Beverley Crown Barker! The second reason I can remember this incident is the sequel to his falling in the sea and being dragged out. We all came into the classroom and Miss Wilson, the infant teacher, set him on top of a stool with tears and sea–water streaming from him. She asked if anyone had any spare clothes that he could wear. Now one of the boys, Denis Aim, had a pair of dungarees on top of his short trousers and offered these. What happened then was rather amusing. The teacher said, 'Now I want you all to sit there with your eyes tightly closed while I remove Richard's wet trousers and put on a dry pair. DON'T OPEN YOUR EYES UNTIL I TELL YOU!' We all closed our eyes but I have to confess that, like every other pupil I am sure, I peeped through narrow slits to see what was going on!

I wonder where Richard Beverley Crown Barker is today and other English boys of that time - Peter Armstrong, Donald Williams and Terence Hartley?

The close presence of the sea brings to mind another story. One day I had finished my work and was sitting with my arms folded in the accustomed fashion when the teacher, in this case Mrs. Yorston, gave me a reward for being finished first.

'Take the waste paper basket Gregor and throw it on the shore.' I was pleased to be chosen to do this and went off down the corridor. As I went I took a good look at the basket itself which was pretty badly broken around the rim and thought again what the teacher had said. She had definitely said, 'Throw the waste paper basket on the shore.'

Just to make sure, I retraced my steps, opened the classroom door and enquired in a small voice, 'Please miss will I throw the basket too?'

'No, you silly boy!' came the retort and all the pupils burst out laughing. I can't recall getting any more jobs to do!

The point of telling this story is to make us think for a moment how in the old days we polluted our beautiful islands. Imagine taking the waste-paper bin and dumping it on the shore! Orcadians had regularly seen the shoreline and the sea, even the lochs as dumping grounds. When I first came to Stenness School I was horrified to find that all the swill from the school kitchen was regularly taken away and dumped at the edge of the Stenness Loch! I soon put a stop to that!

My concern with pollution led me to my first project with Stenness School pupils in 1975. As a practical exercise I transported all the pupils to Warbeth Beach at Stromness and asked them to bag every piece of litter that they came across. At that time dumping at sea was in its heyday and we brought back to school many bags of sea-borne litter. As an exercise in geography the pupils now had to look for information on the litter to determine the country in which it had originated and put a sticker on a world map. They then drew graphs of their results. When it came to interpreting the results however practically every pupil drew the conclusion that Norway was the filthiest country in the world for its graph was by far the highest! We were able to show that it could be dangerous to rely on statistics if we did not know the facts. It was simpler to say that there were more Norwegian ships in the North Atlantic than any other!

I have already told some stories about the well known Stenness man Willie Farquhar. One day my brother was cycling back from Houton in Orphir. It was a day of driving rain blown by a strong north wind. When he came to the Brig o Waithe he was exhausted and thought that he would pop into Willie Farquhar's for a cup of tea. He had never been in Willie's before. Willie obliged with a cup of strong tea and a generous helping of condensed milk. Willie liked to know who his customers were however and after trying out all kinds of tricks to reveal the identity of the new visitor he remarked in despair, 'Weel thoo'l be like mesael, thoo'll hae a name!'

During the war Orcadians were warned to keep a lookout for suspicious individuals and it is not surprising that many became obsessed by tales of spies appearing in the islands. There is no doubt that a Fleet Air Arm training programme for officers contributed to this. In this programme officers were dropped off in the darkness in isolated spots and were required to return to camp unnoticed, their final task being to breach the security of the Royal Naval Air Station at Hatston. The sight of such men lurking round farms as they made their way back must have caused Orcadians great anxiety for they knew nothing of such operations. This background has to be understood to appreciate this tale told me by Ian Blair, a war-time fighter pilot based at Skeabrae.

In 1944 he crash landed his Spitfire on Stronsay. He had just shot down an intruding Messerschmitt but fragments of the disintegrating aircraft had struck the Spitfire fuselage and had forced it to ditch. Luckily the Spitfire pilot emerged from the wreckage with only a bleeding nose and made his way slowly over to the nearby house. Mrs. Miller of Yearnasetter was mixing hen's meat when there was a knock at the door. When she answered, there stood the pilot, a bit shocked, his face covered in blood and with harness dangling from him.

'Could you help me?' he asked.

Mrs. Miller took one look at him, 'Yir a spy,' she said.

'Oh no I'm not,' he said.

'I think yir a spy.'

'No, I'm a British pilot. I have just crashed behind your house.'

Mrs Miller was still not convinced.

'Look,' he says, 'come round the corner with me, I'll show you the RAF roundel on the side of the fuselage. If I were German it would have a cross.'

She came round the corner, had a good look at the plane and had another good look at him.

'Weel than', she said, 'come inside'.

'After that,' the pilot said, 'Mrs Miller and the neighbours could not have been more helpful!'

Following on from the story above, a group of young naval officers from Hatston was driven out in the darkness and released at an isolated spot. They were required to get back to base as quickly as possible. One officer told me that he soon discovered he was in Orphir and made his way to a farm which turned out to be Smoogro. There, after identifying himself, he was welcomed by the Cloustons, given a cup of hot steaming tea and to his complete surprise, a banana! I have often wondered how Smoogro folk could have been eating bananas when such fruit was unknown in Britain during the war years!

Did you do Latin at school? If not, the only Latin word you need to know to understand this tale is *semper* which means 'always'.

It was told me by a Royal Naval pilot whose squadron of Seafires was based at Grimsetter during the war. The Commanding Officer asked his pilots to think of a suitable crest for the squadron and to suggest an appropriate Latin motto. A Latin motto might seem to have been a tall order for a pilot but we should remember that many of them were ex-public school or ex-grammar school boys anyway and would have had a good foundation in the language.

Some set about the exercise seriously, others adopted a more light hearted approach. The squadron had had quite a few casualties and several aircraft had been written off which prompted one pilot to use as the basis of his motto SEMPER IN EXCRETA. I shall leave it to the reader's imagination to visualise what the proposed squadron crest looked like.

The suggestions were rejected!

At the turn of the century everyone was excited about the prospect of flying through the air after the first heavier than air machine made its successful flight.

A simple minded Evie man believed that he had the solution to man-powered flight and one winter spent a long time manufacturing large wings out of heather cowes bound together and to these he fixed leather straps. Those who saw his workmanship marvelled at how well crafted the wings were.

He announced his flight day and many neighbours gathered round helping him to fix his wings on his arms. It all looked so professional that they began to wonder after all whether John Willie (we'll call him) did possess outstanding aeronautical knowledge.

He climbed to the top of the byre with great difficulty stood on the pinnacle of the gable end for some time (probably praying!) then calling 'Cheerie bye' over his shoulder to the assembled company he launched himself from the roof. However the weight of his body was such that his wings did not flap even once. He plummeted earthwards disappearing from sight and there was a loud sound, a bit like a gigantic spoonful of clapshot being thrown on to an enormous plate. They ran round the corner to see John Willie's wings sticking vertically out of the iper in the midden with a coughing and spluttering head lodged between them!

Living about the same time as the Evie aviator was a Dounby eccentric, an expert with a soldering iron but his technical skill was greater than his knowledge of structural engineering. He designed and made a bicycle frame and forks entirely from old cocoa tins. Several local folk gathered round the house for his first test drive. He straddled the bicycle and moved off gingerly to everyone's amazement. There was wonder in their eyes as gradually he picked up speed. But roads in those days did not have the velvet smooth surface of today. He hit a small pothole, the forks and frame completely buckled and bicycle and rider collapsed on to the road.

Whit a peety! Most of the great bicycle names of today had their origins at that time in little sheds just like his. With a bit more technical knowledge, who knows, Dounby today might have been the centre of a thriving cycle manufacturing industry!

As a child I cannot remember getting any Christmas presents. I expect that this was true of most children in the 1940s. There was a war on and anyway few families could not afford to buy presents. But there was another factor. Christmas was like any other day in Orkney at that time. In our family the only thing that set it apart was that we had a hen for dinner!

I was shocked to hear on the radio the other day the manager of one of Britain's largest stores say that nowadays it is not uncommon for parents to spend £700 on a child at Christmas! A typical present would be a top of the range mountain bike. The pressure on parents today to keep up with other parents must be enormous but is not entirely new as we learn from a story about a Rendall family in the early 1900s.

At that time cycle racing was a very popular pastime and every boy wanted a bike. A visitor to the Rendall household reported the following conversation:-

Son: Fither I want a bicycle and I want her the morn and if sheu doesna baet Ah'll brak her.

Father: Oh my Johno buddo thoo're no gan tae get a bicycle if thoor're gan tae brak her.

I wonder how much father would have paid for his son's bike in those days - probably the equivalent of £1.50!

I am told that fifty per cent of Christmas presents are sold, passed on or donated to charity. We have all received Christmas presents which we have not particularly liked but we should always show appreciation. When a present comes from a member of the family with an expectation that it will be displayed or used it is particularly difficult if the present does not have any appeal. When such a present comes from a young daughter to a father, a dilemma can arise. A Stenness man was given a present of after-shave lotion in such circumstances. He took a sniff of the contents, smiled and (obligingly) declared that it was just what he wanted. After the Christmas holidays he applied it liberally to his face and proudly let his daughter smell his cheeks before he set off to work. On the bus gaan tae the toon he sat beside a colleague who, after a few pleasantries, said

'Whit's that smell wae yi the day beuy?' 'Oh,' he said with some embarrassment, 'hid 's after-shave me dowter gid me for Christmas and I felt I hid tae pit hid oan for her sake.' 'Oh beuy, ' said the fellow passenger, 'for mercy sake don't pit that stuff oan again - yi smell like a hoor's handbag.'

One of my classmates at an evening class in Somerset was a policeman. He had served almost thirty years in the service and was about to retire. One evening in the interval between classes we were swopping stories. He told me that when he first went on highway patrol his instructor said that a useful opening remark to a speeding motorist was, 'Right mate, where's the fire?'

Shortly after his introduction to patrol duties he had just come down a side road and was about to join the main road when a car shot past in excess of 80 mph. He gave chase with his blue light flashing and the speeding car pulled in. He strode confidently up to the driver and gave him a sign to wind down his window.

'Right mate, where's the fire?' he asked.

'Woolworth's in town,' came the reply.

He had stopped a fireman!

I told this story to my brother, a former policeman who, in turn, told me another version of this story.

A highway patrolman in America stopped a speeding motorist on the freeway. He got out of his car and approached the offending vehicle. The window was run down to reveal an absolutely beautiful looking woman the sight of whom slightly disarmed him.

'Right, ma'm,' he said, 'where's the fire?'

She threw back her golden hair and looked at him through half-closed fluttering eyelids, 'In your eyes officer,' she said.

A geology professor taking a tutorial held up a piece of rock and said, 'This sample is three hundred million and twenty one years old.'

A sceptical student interrupted, 'How can you possibly date that rock so accurately?' he asked.

'Well,' said the professor, 'I started my academic career in this department as a young man. In my first year I held up this same piece of rock and I told my students then that it was three hundred million years old – and that was twenty one years ago!'

I speak for many teachers and lecturers when I say that coming across a terrible piece of work we are frequently loath to read it to the end. It is tempting to jump over a few pages to reach the end more quickly.

A history student at Edinburgh was awarded a very poor mark for an essay and had the distinct impression that it hadn't been properly read. Next time he thought he would trick the professor. Before he handed in his essay he put a tiny spot of glue between each page.

The essay was returned to his pigeon hole some weeks later with a very low grade. Flicking through the pages he found to his delight that all the glue seals remained intact. As he walked along the corridor he saw the professor coming towards him and cheerfully challenged him.

'Professor,' he said, 'you have given me another very poor mark for my essay and you haven't even read all of it – look, all the glue seals that I placed between the pages are still intact.'

'Well my boy,' said the professor unruffled, 'one does not need to eat the whole of an egg to know that it is bad.'

Did you have a 'comforter' when you were little – a dirty piece of old blanket which went everywhere with you, the one corner blackened with a mixture of saliva and dirt? Orkney folk call them a 'sookie'. Children all over the world carry such things. Recently on film I saw a little Japanese child with one; there it's probably called a suzuki.

While an Englishman is thinking of an answer to a question he will say, 'Mmmmmmmmmmm....'

While an Orcadian is thinking of an answer to a question he will say, 'Ehhhhhhh....'

I had not been in Birmingham very long when I went to an ironmonger and asked him if he could match the key which I put on the counter.

'Yes,' he said, 'how many do you want?'

Before I made a decision he disappeared, much to my surprise. He returned immediately and put eight identical keys on the counter.

'What's that for?' I asked.

'You said you wanted eight,' he replied.

'No I didn't,' I said, 'I hadn't still made up my mind when you disappeared. I want only one actually.'

'Could have sworn you said eight,' he said.

I laughed as much as to say that I hadn't even spoken.

As I walked away from the shop I realised that I must have said 'Ehhhhhhhhhhh...' which he interpreted as ' eight' and that's why he disappeared!

We lived outside the city of Glasgow for some time in a fairly new house. We hadn't been there very long until we became aware of the fact that the roof leaked very badly. One really hot summer's day I decided it would be a good opportunity to investigate the leaking roof. I borrowed the neighbour's ladder and began to strip tiles off the offending area. It soon became apparent what was wrong – a combination of a broken tile near a roof channel and a very badly felted piece underneath with exposed sarking. I had to get some felt for a start to solve the problem and a new tile if I could. For this I had to drive into the outskirts of Glasgow. I left the roof as it was, jumped in the car and set off.

Although the weather was beautiful when I set off, as I made my way through the traffic the sky got darker and darker. Having reached my destination I parked the car as near as possible to the merchant's and began to run down the street. As I did so, there was a vivid flash of lightning and a deafening peal of thunder followed by torrential rain.

I took refuge in a bus shelter along with an elderly gentleman who welcomed me with the words, 'This is worse than affa!' which I found very amusing.

I continued the conversation by saying, 'It would be a day like this that I have a hole in my roof, wouldn't it?'

He looked up at me quizzically, 'Ye have a hole in your roof sur?' he asked, 'that'll be the Cooncil.'

I made an appropriate reply hinting that it was the Council's fault but I said to myself with a smile, 'Where else but Glasgow would one hear a remark like that!'

Trams while they lasted were my favourite means of city transport. However when I got my own scooter some years afterwards and the tram lines were still down on the streets of Aberdeen I cursed them for it was very easy to lose control of one's machine if the front wheel went into a tram line – especially in wet conditions.

A friend told me the amusing story of wet Glasgow tramlines. The reader will need to know that trams in Glasgow were called 'cors', i.e. 'cars'.

A tramdriver had to brake suddenly when something suddenly went across his path. The following vehicle travelling at too great a speed braked but slid into the tramlines and carried on, crashing into the back of the tram with a resounding wallop.

The tram conductress or clippie (always celebrated for their wit) leaned out of the partly demolished back of the tram and shouted at the driver, 'How do you sto-ap when there are nae cors aboot?'

In the first quarter of last century a man who farmed in Firth was not of native stock. He was not a very good farmer either and one of his neighbours told him frankly what he thought about his crop.

'Thee oats are aal growan in busses min.'

The farmer scanned his field and with a snort replied, 'Frankly man I don't give a damn if they are growing in tramcars!'

Last year I became an unwitting accomplice in a trick. It happened in this way. I rang my insurance company about an outstanding claim.

'Mr Lamb speaking,' I said, 'could you put me through to Claims.'

'Certainly sir, ringing for you.'

The telephone was picked up in the Claims Department.

'Morning Mr Sheep,' a voice said.

I was a bit surprised. 'It's Mr. <u>Lamb</u> actually.'

'Oh Mr Lamb I'm terribly, terribly sorry. Please accept my <u>sincere</u> apologies. I'll get that damn joker on reception. How can I help?'

I had a good laugh to myself; I only wish I knew the sequel to that conversation!

The old red telephone boxes have such heavy doors. When Kirkwall Telephone Exchange was in operation a 999 call came in one Saturday night and the telephonist enquired in the usual manner, 'Fire Police or Ambulance?' An inebriated voice at the end of the line said, 'Can yi tell me the wey tae git oot o this 'phone box?'

There's an old Orkney cure for a smoking fire as we learn from this tale.

A West Mainland blacksmith was making a piece for an open fire one day with the customer standing beside him. When he had finished the customer said, 'Beuy thoo're made a good job o that. Feth are thoo. Noo can thoo tell me whit wey tae stop me fire fae reekan?'

'Ah'll tell thee a owld cure for a reekan fire,' the blacksmith said, 'tak a flooer pot min and hing hid in thee lum and thoo'll niver hiv any more trouble.'

'That'll niver work,' said the customer.

'Weel hid generally does,' said the blacksmith.

The customer said that he would try it anyway because he was fed up of sitting in a house full of blue reek.

A month later the man came back to the smithy.

'Is thee fire ventan any better noo wi the flooer pot in hid?' asked the blacksmith.

'No wan whit better,' said the man and with a wry smile added, 'and forbye hid's killed the wife 's flooer.'

In those days before Automatic Telephone Exchanges, every telephone call had to go through an exchange. There the operator would ask 'Number please?' On busy exchanges some telephone operators became almost demented after saying 'number please' thousands of times a day so they had little tricks up their sleeves to retain their sanity. Instead of saying 'number please' for example they would say 'rubber knees'; this would be followed by a short pause in which the caller wondered whether he had heard correctly! When it came to saying 'trying to connect you', the operator would substitute 'dying to collect you'.

A girl student in Edinburgh was telephoning her parents on the Harray exchange.

'Could you put me through to Harray, please?' In this instance the male operator must also have been a little bored.

'Sorry, my dear,' he said, 'Harry's already with a woman – but Bill's a nice chap – will he do?'

The Highland train service between Inverness and Thurso was famous for being so slow. I can remember that the train would stop at every small station while the guard got out to deliver the morning paper!

A businessman standing on the platform at Dingwall station checked his watch from time to time and looked anxiously up the line to see whether there was any sign of the train. After some time he began to pace up and down the platform watched by a smiling fellow traveller who, after a short while, was able to go over and reassure the businessman of the train's imminent arrival.

'The train won't be long now,' he said in crisp Highland tones, 'I can see the driver's dog coming down the line.'

Much time is spent in school, and rightly so, in establishing the correct meanings of words. In a class test in a Midlands primary school pupils were asked to give the exact meaning of a list of words which included the word 'legend'. The teacher was puzzled by the answer 'foot' in one instance until he realised that the pupil had read the word as 'leg-end'.

I was doing reading in a one to one relationship with a pupil in Stenness Primary School when we came across the word 'custodian'. I asked the pupil what it meant. He scratched his head.

'I don't know,' he replied.

'See if we can work it out from the context,' I went on. But this approach did not work.

'If I say 'Maeshowe' to you is that any help?' I asked,

'Ah,' he said, 'I know - DRAGON!'

I told this story to the Maeshowe custodian of the time and she was not amused!

Norway, Sweden and Denmark are usually thrown together as one big land mass called Scandinavia and this leads us to believe that they are all one big, unified group of people. Nothing can be further from the truth. Norwegians think the Swedes are snobs and Swedes poke fun at the Norwegians - especially at their language. Sweden has a long established official language but Norwegians can't make up their mind what their language should be. And so the story goes that a Norwegian went to work in the office of a Swedish forestry company. Two Swedes in the company were talking of the new recruit and the conversation went like this:-

'There's a Norwegian in the office, downstairs.'

'Oh.'

'They say he can speak five languages.'

'Five languages?'

'Yes - and four of them are Norwegian.'

I have long been in touch with an American who is very proud of his Orkney ancestry. I visited him some years ago and he told me an amusing story.

He lives in Los Angeles and is in charge of sales for a large swathe of

USA. Frequently he and his colleagues host businessmen from all over the world. On this occasion they were hoping to do business with the Finnish firm Nokia and he and the negotiating team had brought the representative to a fine restaurant.

They found to their embarrassment during the starter course that the Finn was a painfully slow eater, talking the whole time in quite bad English. They wondered what would happen during the main course. Their worst fears were confirmed. They tried to eat as slowly as their guest but it was no use - the food just became horribly cold so they emptied their plates and sat and waited. The Finn was oblivious to the embarrassment he was causing while the waiters were pacing up and down behind his table ready to swoop.

At one point the Finn had this very exciting story to tell which involved the use of his hands and he laid down his knife and fork on the plate.

At this the waiter leaned over his shoulder and said, 'Are you finished, sir.'

The man looked up in surprise, smiled and said, 'Yes I am Finnish,' whereupon the waiter grabbed his half-full plate and made off!

From films we learn how parade sergeants like to bark out the surnames of new recruits. In the Royal Navy certain ratings are always referred to by their superiors by their first name on the very first day of service and forever after. Such ratings have the common English surnames 'Darling' and 'Love'! Hardly anyone on board a naval vessel is called by his/her proper name; before long someone thinks of a nickname. A rating had the unusual surname 'Granite'. After some time this rating was promoted to Petty Officer in Mechanical Engineering and his new rank was P/O, M/E Granite. Henceforth he was always known as 'Pomegranate.'

I told a friend about an Orkney girl whose married name was Sunniva Gunn. He told me of a colleague who had a daughter called Teresa. She married someone with the surname 'Green' and her new name became Teresa Green which everyone understood as 'trees are green'!

My brother and his wife gave some thought to christening their son 'Alistair'. 'Alistair Lamb' sounded a fine strong name which could not be twisted easily into any nickname. Unfortunately Alistair hadn't been to school very long until he was nicknamed 'Ally' by some of his classmates and 'Ba' by others. After a few weeks both nicknames were joined together to become Ali Ba Ba and at the age of 50 remains so today!

One day a family of rabbits who lived at the Hammers o Syraday in Firth decided they needed a break. Father thought that some time at the Bay o Skaill on the links there would be fine. So they made preparations to set off. Father would lead the way, Peedie Breeks would carry the sandwiches and at Billy Wylie's they would stop for lemonade which mum would carry. Off they set. Their first stop was at the Harray Stores where Dad bought some Cream Soda. Peedie Breeks was already thirsty and wanted a drink immediately but dad would not allow this.

'No lemonade till we get tae Skaill,' he said, 'noo mither, you cairry hid. Ah'll laed the wey again. Right! Off we go!'

Peedie Breeks pootsed and fell ahint and almost got struck by one of Isbister's big cattle trucks on hid's wey to the Mart as he crossed the main road in front of Billy Wylie's.

'Right,' said dad, 'up to the front here wi me beuy. Ah'm no hivan any of this insolence.'

Peedie Breeks did what he was told. Off northwards they set, past Kirkness Farm, round the edge of the loch, by Housegarth and so down to the Bay o Skaill. My what a grand day it was and what fun they were going to have.

'First we'll need tae hiv some refreshments,' said Dad, 'shaa me the lemonade mither.'

'There yi are.'

'And Peedie Breeks the sandwiches noo.'

'The sandwiches? Oh my, fither, Ah'm sorry I don't seem to hiv the sandwiches.'

'Yi whit?'

'I don't seem to have the sandwiches. I must hiv left them at the petrol pumps at Billy Wylie's when we were hivan the argument aboot the lemonade.'

'Right beuy, yir gan tae learn yir lesson. We sit here and you go straight back for them.'

'Oh no Ah'm no, for when I go yi'll both drink the lemonade; hid's no fair!'

'No we'll no. We'll sit here and wait till you come back. Noo aff you go and be queek aboot hid.'

Peedie Breeks was not one to argue with his father. He hopped over a sand dune and disappeared.

Mum and dad now sat down and waited… and waited. Hours passed, then days, days turned into a week.

Eventually Mum said, 'I don't think he's coman back.'

'No,' said Dad, 'doesna luk like hid. Likely got hit bae that Isbister's truck coman back fae the Mart.'

'Yaas,' said Mum, 'poor peedie Peedie Breeks.'

Dad began to unscrew the top of the Cream Soda bottle.

'Weel mither, we'll hiv a drink furtiverweys.'

'Might as weel,' said Mum.

Dad had just lifted the bottle to his lips when a little voice called from behind the sand dune, 'Don't drink that lemonade or Ah'll no go!'

In secondary school we had a teacher who shall be nameless. His 'lessons' regularly went like this:-

'Open your books at page….You at the back, will you begin reading at the top of the page.'

In this way the 'lesson' would begin, punctuated by the teacher shouting from time to time 'Next…..next…..next'. Meanwhile the teacher himself got on with reading a novel - or even *The Orcadian* I remember on one occasion.

The pupils got a bit fed up with this; they were convinced that the teacher wasn't even listening to their reading. One boy in another class set out to prove it. At the end of every sentence he introduced the word 'wheelbarrow'. He had managed five sentences and had succeeded in uttering the word 'wheelbarrow' five times when the teacher raised his head slowly from his book.

'Sinclair!' he said, 'where are all these damned wheelbarrows coming from?'

During the war it was impossible to travel north of Inverness unless one had a special pass. The North of Scotland was a Protected Zone. Such trains were heaving with service personnel and a WREN travelling north to Twatt Royal Naval Air Station spent most of the journey sitting on her kitbag in the corridor. After some time a young mother with a little baby came out of the toilet. She set her suitcase down in the corridor and took up position beside the WREN. After some time the WREN learned that her fellow traveller was indeed a stowaway! She had locked herself in the toilet and the guards on this occasion had failed to check it. She had emerged when the train had started. And her mission? She explained that she had finally learned where the father of her child, a naval airman, was based – he was stationed at Hatston. She intended to cause him severe embarrassment by walking into the station and confronting him in front of his superior officers with the baby! She often wondered what the outcome of the girl's mission was!

Don't read this little bit if you are eating for it deals with a very unpleasant subject. When a cat makes a mess in the house, why does it always go into a corner? Why doesn't it do it right in the middle of the floor – it's so much easier to clean up. Not only that, it can be easily and immediately seen and does not lie unnoticed for days. It must be something built into our genes which makes animals – and that includes us – go into corners if we have anything to evacuate. When I was quite small I was in W B Firth's shop in Finstown with my older sister. We had been sent down for messages. The shop was busy and we were standing in the middle of the floor waiting our turn. Suddenly I became very hot and my mouth kept filling up with water. I said to my sister, 'Ah'm gan tae be seek!'

'You canna be seek in here,' she said, 'had hid in!'

Now that is quite a challenge for a peedie boy. Up it came, I pressed my lips together, my cheeks bulged but the lips held firm and I waited. I hoped the shop assistant didn't ask me what we wanted!

But I couldn't cope with the next surge – I dashed to the corner of the shop and lost it all in a great explosion. Unfortunately that's where Stanley Firth stored all the walking sticks! What a disgusting mess the assistant had to clean up – imagine wiping down all these walking sticks too. I remember her saying to my sister, 'Could he no done hid in the middle o the floor?!'

Still on this very unpleasant subject I was driving along a dusty road in Turkey many years ago in an old Volkswagen Beetle. It was a lovely day and for those of you who have never driven such a car, the windscreen wipers weren't very good. Why would I need windscreen wipers on a lovely day you might ask. Just wait.

Suddenly I was overtaken by a coach travelling at quite a speed. In the old days these coaches quite often had a rear door which was used normally only in emergencies. Just as it passed I saw the rear door open.

'What's going on here?' I asked myself.

I was soon to find out. A man leaned out and was violently sick. The sickness swirled in the slipstream of the coach for a minute then went SPLAT! right on my windscreen. I was travelling at about 40 mph at the time and all of a sudden I could see nothing! I switched on my windscreen wipers which heaved and groaned under the strain while I tried my best to control the car. Then the smell of sickness came into the car and you know what effect that has! Finally I was able to bring the car safely to a halt and I had this disgusting mess to clean away. Whoever the culprit was he should have been charged with dangerous spewing!

Doctors must have some brilliant stories to tell about their patients! Of course we don't normally hear of them for such conversations are rightly confidential. However I was fortunate enough to hear a tale from the Dounby Surgery - from the patient's point of view!

An old Birsay man told me about an amusing visit he had to the Dounby doctor. He had been to the doctor's for his usual annual check up and the doctor was delighted with his continued good health.

'I've thoroughly examined you Mr Spence (we'll call him)', he said. 'You seem to be in pretty good shape for your age. No blood pressure problems and you have the heart of a fifty year old man.'

'Ah'm playsed tae hear that,' replied Mr Spence.

'Now,' the doctor continued, 'is there anything I don't know about? Anything worrying you that I may have an answer for?'

'I hiv aafil trouble wi me feet nooadays.'

'Trouble with your feet? In what way?' the doctor asked.

'Ah'm kinda shakky on them and when Ah'm waalkan ap tae the hoose noo for instance I canna white keekan me feet in busses o gress. Wid yi hiv a answer tae that?'

'Certainly Mr Spence, I could prescribe something to eliminate that.'

'Whit wid that be – tablets?'

'No', replied the doctor, 'I suggest Mr Spence that you just lift your feet a little higher.'

During the war Fleet Air Arm aircraft would frequently be seen in the skies of Orkney dragging far behind them a canvas cylinder known as a 'drogue'. These drogues acted as targets for Royal Naval and sometimes for RAF gunners. Occasionally rogue drogues would break loose and fall from the sky and of course the Royal Navy wanted them back. A reward of £3 was offered for their return to Twatt or Hatston, a very generous reward, about the same as the weekly wage of a County Council worker at the time! A drogue was therefore a valuable find.

As two children were coming home from Oxtro School they saw a drogue falling from the sky into a field. They hopped over the dyke and ran to retrieve it. However as they were running towards it they saw the farmer on whose land the drogue had landed running as fast as he could to get his hands on it. The children got there first and started to pull it towards the dyke but then the farmer caught up with them, got hold of it and started to pull it towards his house.

'Laeve hid alone, hid's on me land!' he bawled at them.

'We got hid first! Hid's wirs!' they shouted back but the teams were unevenly matched in this tug-of-war and the farmer started to pull drogue and children in his direction.

Meanwhile other children passing on the road saw what was happening; all of them jumped over the dyke too and an almighty tug of war began. But the farmer was no match for the hordes of children and after being dragged in the direction of the school for some time gave up and walked home – no doot wi his tail atween his legs!

A Fleet Air Arm Observer stationed at Twatt during the war told me that on a cold winter's day they took off in a Boston to do Radar Calibration. Shortly after the aircraft took off they were caught in a violent rainstorm. He wasn't aware that the aircraft leaked and worked busily at his instruments. Soon they had broken through the cloud and were flying at high altitude in beautiful weather but at 20 degrees Fahrenheit it was bitterly cold. He thought it was a good job he was wearing a flying jacket and flying boots to keep him warm. On return to base when he attempted to get out of the aircraft he found it difficult. The rain had poured into the footwell of his seat and at high altitude had formed into a frozen block trapping his feet!

A North Isles lady was not very happy about her new neighbours fae sooth. The bairns made a terrible noise and sometimes to her annoyance a football would come over the wall and land in her vegetable plot. Eventually she would hurl insults at them with the result that, in the end the bairns were frightened to knock on the door and ask for their ball back. The father, a very polite man, said that he would go and ask for the ball. 'I'm terribly sorry Mrs I....... but could I have the children's ball back – it's gone over the wall again'. Mrs I....... looked at him fiercely, 'The next time this b★★★★★ thing comes intae me gairden Ah'm gaan tae burst hid. And by the wey hid's no a wall, hid's a b★★★★★ dyke!'

I remember a long time ago reading a tale about William Wordsworth. He had looked down on a lakeland village musing about the idyllic life of the villagers. However when he got to know the village at a later date he found that far from being a haven of peace and tranquillity, the villagers were all at each others' throats!

I am amused when I read in *The Orcadian* newspaper letters from sooth country visitors saying what a lot of fine peaceable folk Orcadians are. A few years spent in Orkney might change that point of view! There are parts of Orkney where the bitterest feelings exist between neighbours sometimes passing down through several generations. When I was collecting Orkney dialect words I was given a good example of this by an informant who supplied me with the word *choomheed*. I quote from *Orkney Wordbook*:–

> **choomheed** a stupid fool. In an argument in Shapinsay in the 1880s a man dismissed three generations of his neighbour's family in one sentence, '*Min thoo are a choomheed and so thoo are and so wis thee fither afore thee and luk at thee son Willie, whit a choomheed he is.*'

Someone in every parish can tell a tale of farmers whose lands lie side by side and yet who don't speak to each other. In one parish two brothers with adjacent farms have not spoken to each other for many years. In another instance the ownership of a field which was the subject of a legal dispute was never resolved. It is said that one of these farmers taunted the other by placing a very large stone in the middle of the disputed field. The other, assuming that this was evidence of possession removed it under the cover of darkness!

What is the first part of *The Orcadian* that you read? Many turn first of all to the births and deaths column! But can you imagine reading this column and finding your own name in it! This happened at one time to a South Isles man. Forty years ago a South Ronaldsay man hated his neighbour so much that he wished he was dead. He got carried away with this idea and successfully inserted an announcement in The *Orcadian* to the effect that his neighbour had passed away!

Perhaps the worst instance of bad neighbourliness comes from Sandwick where there was a fierce dispute between two farmers over the right of way to a well by the name of 'Plunko'. Farmer A claimed that his family had an inalienable right to pass over the land of Farmer B to reach the well. One day when the wife of Farmer A came to draw water she discovered that Farmer B had settled the argument once and for all. She found to her disgust that, under cover of darkness, he had used it as a toilet!

So yi see wir no aal that different fae ither folk!

Writing about the South Ronaldsay man who reported the death of his neighbour brings to mind another similar story. When I wrote the book *Sky Over Scapa*, I included a section on wartime air accidents in Orkney. Such information was extremely difficult to obtain but as I found out when I began researching the book, the world is full of experts on all aspects of military aviation. What a friendly lot of people they are too, all willing to share their knowledge. It was through them that much of the section on air accidents was built up. The interesting thing about Fleet Air Arm accidents is that practically all the war time records were destroyed in the post-war period by an over-zealous officer who wanted some shelf space. Most of the information we have today has been collected from personal reminiscence and as can be imagined, small inaccuracies have crept in here and there.

Shortly after the book was published I had a letter from a gentleman in Dorset. He began by quoting Mark Twain, 'the report of my death was an exaggeration....' The letter was from a Fleet Air Arm pilot who, according to my book, had been killed in an aircraft crash in Orkney! Fortunately he knew the background to the difficulties in collecting records and was very understanding. He had in fact been in a very serious accident, his Hurricane coming down on the perimeter of Skeabrae, hitting a henhouse and disintegrating. How he got out alive, he doesn't know. To give some idea of the state of the aircraft, his flying helmet was found caught on the tailplane!

How could I reply to such a letter I asked myself? Perhaps I could begin with a quotation too – an apologetic quotation. The perfect quotation which I found also happened to be from Mark Twain. My letter began, 'There was things which he stretched but mainly he told the truth.'

An old Shetland man was digging a hole in the ground for a post when a neighbour came along.

'Min yir hivan a hard job there.'

'Aye,' he says, 'hit says in the good book that the Lord made the warld in sax days. Consideran the short time he tuk, hit's weel pitten taegither.'

I have earlier spoken of my former neighbour Robbie. Such a fine old man; God rest his soul! He loved a dram and on the odd occasion sometimes had one for breakfast. But not for him the gentle sip. As the following story relates, his whisky disappeared as swiftly as a Russian would dispose of his vodka. One day he and an old friend went into a bar in Kirkwall. The friend whom I knew well was an equally likable man but very slow in his speech and his actions. The friend ordered two double whiskies which were set on the counter.

'Wid thoo like watter in thee whisky Robbie?' the friend asked then looking down at the counter remarked in astonishment, 'good min thoo're doan wi thee whisky!'

In the late 1930s my sister Edna was having a meal with a Kirkwall family. She took her place at the table beside 'Auntie' who was something of a hypochondriac. To Edna's surprise 'Auntie' produced three little bottles from her handbag. Two tablets were removed from each and set on the table beside her.

'Whit's the tablets for?' enquired Edna.

'Weel that wans are for me haert,' said 'Auntie' pointing, 'I hiv tae tak them afore me dinner; this wans are for me stimmach and I tak them when Ah'm eatan and this wans are for a liver complaint and I tak them when Ah'm done wi me dinner.'

Edna was amazed, 'My,' she asked, 'hoo dae they aal ken whar tae go?'

I was told the story of George, a Dorset farmer, who always helped his neighbour Benjamin whenever he could. One day George arrived to lend a hand with the hay but the neighbour said, 'There be no haymakin today; he goin to rain'.

'He not goin to rain,' said George, 'on my weather gauge the lady she be out and the man he be in. My grandfather and his father before him swore by that weather gauge; I tell ee; it be a fine day for haymakin'.

So George and Benjamin set off to the fields to turn the hay. After an hour the sky darkened, the wind rose and it began to pour with rain.

'Told ee so,' said Benjamin picking up his jacket and making tracks for the farmhouse..

A disconcerted George scratched his head and set off home.

The first thing he did was to have a good look at his weather gauge. No he hadn't made a mistake; the lady was out and the man was in.

He climbed on a chair, took the weather gauge off the wall and had a good look at it. There was the explanation! The man couldn't get out! He was firmly trapped by a big spider's web!

Old Mrs Davidson (we'll call her) from Stenness was a hypochondriac. She always seemed to have something wrong with her and was forever calling the doctor. Where most people had china dogs and tea caddies on their mantelpiece Mrs Davidson's was bowed down with the weight of medicine bottles. She was rather plump and the doctor told her that if she were to lose weight she would feel a lot better and wouldn't have so many aches and pains. But Mrs. Davidson 'liked her maet' as she said and there was some doubt about how she could get her weight down.

'A diet,' the doctor said, 'a diet would be the solution.'

Mrs Davidson was a little hard of hearing by this time and of course always being concerned about her food, asked the doctor, 'Will I hiv tae tak this 'diet thing' afore me maet or efter?'

Magnus Spence, the great Orkney naturalist and author of *Flora Orcadensis* tells the story of one day he was taking one of his customary nature walks.

An acquaintance came up to him as he walked along a hill path, 'Whit are yi deuan the day min?' he asked.

'Ah'm gaetheran flooers,' Magnus replied.

'Gaetheran flooers?' he enquired in disbelief.

'Yaas.'

The man laughed, 'Min that's the wark o feuls and bairns,' he said!

An old chapel site in Evie is called the Kirk o Buggery. The origin of the word in this context is not known. An old farm in Stenness was called Dams and its incumbent at one time was referred to in typical friendly Orkney fashion as Tam o the Dams. Sometimes he was called (in a manner no less friendly) Tam o the Buggers.

I have always been intrigued by the attitude of incoming children to Orkney dialect. When I returned to Orkney in 1974 I was astonished to hear two West Indian looking boys in Dounby speaking broad Orkney dialect. Sometime later I heard a little Chinese boy cycling up Albert Street shouting ' Aye beuy!' to a friend!

I noticed in Stenness school that whereas some incoming children did not change their mode of speech in any way others adopted the local dialect very rapidly. They learned to speak the dialect just by listening to their peers and subconsciously forming rules. Orkney dialect has rules for its pronunciation just as English does but like English there are exceptions to the rule. Here is an instance of a pupil wrongly applying a rule he had subconsciously learned.

As part of a project the pupils were taken to Maeshowe. As we stood outside, an English boy who had been in the school a short while looked at Maeshowe and said, 'Beuy this is some <u>moond</u>'. All the pupils laughed at his pronunciation naturally for although practically every 'ou' and indeed 'ow' sound in English is pronounced in dialect as if it were 'oo', 'mound' is not among them! It is pronounced as it is in English. A good rule of thumb in Orkney dialect nevertheless is that all 'ows' and 'ous' are pronounced 'oos'!

When an Orcadian speaks English he has to learn the opposite rule – all 'oos' are not 'ows'! I remember from my early school days being caught out with this. I was asked to read out aloud from my reading book and when I came across the word 'elbow' which in dialect is pronounced 'elboo', I pronounced it to rhyme with 'allow'.

'No you silly boy!' the teacher said, at which point I became a bit flustered and said 'elboo' for which I got a typical 'crack' on the side of the head!

Some Orkney teachers fail to make use of the excellent opportunities presented by a child's use of dialect. An eight year old girl told this story to her parents because she was quite hurt by the teacher's reaction to a boy's answer in class.

The teacher said to the class, 'Who can give me a word which rhymes with 'owl'?

A boy put up his hand. 'Yes, John?'

'Please miss, bowl' (he used dialect pronunciation in which case it did rhyme with 'owl').

'Bowl?' she scoffed (using the same pronunciation), there's no such word'.

What the teacher didn't know is that Orcadians use the original English pronunciation of 'bowl'!

The word 'bowl' should really be spelt 'boll' in English, the present day spelling reflects the old form of pronunciation!

Here is the story of someone 'chantan' and getting his 'oos' and 'ows' confused!

'Cloot' is the Orkney dialect word for 'cloth' used in the sense of 'rag'. For example we would talk of a 'table cloot', or simply 'cloot' meaning a 'dishcloth'.

A Stromness man who held a senior position in town rarely spoke dialect. He always 'chanted'. One evening he was having a dinner party for a select number of his friends. During the course of the evening while telling a story he accidentally knocked over his wine glass.

He called to his wife in the kitchen to say that a dishcloth was required. Normally an Orcadian in his position would have said, 'Mary tak a cloot ben!' but not our man. Chantan badly he shouted 'Mary bring a <u>clowt</u> when you come through.'

We could add to this the tale of the little girl who was asked by a sooth country visitor in the classroom what her name was.

'My name is Edith <u>Clowston</u>,' she replied!

Following on from what has been said a ferrylouper would soon learn that the word 'doubt' is pronounced as if it were 'doot' but having made this step forward he would then learn to his surprise that in Orkney dialect it means the opposite of what it means in English!

Two men, an American and an Englishman were on the Harray Loch fishing with an Orkney ghillie.

The American said, 'Gee folks I think its gonna rain.'

The Orcadian said, 'I doot hid'.

The Englishman said, 'I doubt it.'

At first sight both the Orcadian and the Englishman appeared to be disagreeing with the American but this is was not the case. Whereas the Englishman disagreed with the American, the Orcadian agreed with him! Well it did rain and the Englishman was proved wrong! The real meaning of Orcadian 'I doot' is 'I'm afraid so'. It has the meaning of 'something undesirable which has happened, is happening, will continue or is about to happen'.

An Orkney dialect phrase with similar peculiarities is 'I widna say.' A direct translation of this phrase is ' I wouldn't say' but this is true only if it is used in a sentence e.g. 'I widna say he's as clever as his brither.' However if 'I widna say' is used on its own in a reply to a remark made by someone else, it has a completely different meaning.

Let's go back to the boat on the Harray Loch again and change the conversation a little.

The American said, 'Gee folks I think its gonna rain.'

The Orcadian said, 'I widna say'.

The Englishman said, 'I wouldn't say that.'

In this instance the Orcadian 'I widna say,' means 'I agree with you that there is a very great possibility.... whereas the Englishman disagrees completely!

The real difference between 'I doot hid,' and 'I widna say' is that the former relates only to undesirable outcomes whereas the latter can refer to any kind of outcome!

Here is an amusing story in which 'I doot' is used in the sense of 'something undesirable which will continue'.

A North Isles man who had come into the Mart on a Monday had instructions from his wife to try and buy a new vacuum cleaner for theirs was 'fairly doan'. The assistant was trying to convince the man to buy a Dyson cleaner, one of these ultra-modern machines.

'The great thing aboot this cleaner,' said the assistant, 'is that yi can get rid o the bag.'

'Oh no,' the man replied, 'Ah'll hiv tae keep her I doot.'

When I began collecting old Orkney dialect words in the 1980s a Sanday man wrote to me to say that he was rather confused because when he went to school in the late 1920s he had the Orkney dialect beaten out of him and here was I, a headmaster, actively encouraging its use! I was able to tell my correspondent that I had the dialect beaten out of me too and here's a story to prove it, only this is going one step too far!

The English word 'steak' has a most peculiar pronunciation; anyone learning English would make the reasonable assumption that it should rhyme with 'teak'. However the English pronunciation of 'steak' comes very easily to the Orcadian tongue and sounds very much like the dialect pronunciation 'stek'.

When I came across the word 'steak' written for the first time I concluded that I had been completely mispronouncing it all along and so when I went to the shop for messages I proudly said to the assistant, 'Could I have a pound of steek please.'

'Whit did yi say yi wanted?' she asked.

'A pound of steek,' I repeated.

'Steek?' she said and turning to the other assistant asked, 'whit's steek?'

The other shook her head, 'I don't ken,' she said and then bending down shouted, 'whit are yi wantan beuy?'

'Steek,' I said, then rather flustered shouted, 'maet!'

'Oh,' she said, 'hid's a pund o steak, the boy's wantan.'

After that I stuck to Orkney dialect!

And from that period yet another instance of language conflict which perhaps only an Orcadian can appreciate. When I was a pupil in primary school I was walking home one day with a friend when the class teacher came along the road on her bicycle.

As she passed she shouted ,'Gregor Lamb, your lace is loose.'

I turned to the friend, 'Whit did she say?' I asked.

'She said yir laecer's lowse,' he replied!

Sometimes words will not come out of our mouths in the right order. I remember once reading of a Scots lady who went to the butcher's and said, 'Could I have a fowling boil? Oh dear,' she went on, 'I mean a boiling foil – sorry a fouling bowl.' She could not get 'boiling fowl' out correctly.

Such mistakes can sometimes cause acute embarrassment. A Stenness lady often cycled to the shop for messages on a bonny day. One fine day she decided she would have to take the bus.

'No cyclan the day?' the bus driver enquired.

'No,' she replied, 'Ah'm no cyclan any more till I git me pike bumped.'

And of course the bus was 'fill o folk' which added to the embarrassment.

One of my former Birmingham pupils now teaches in a school for severely disturbed children. I was in conversation with her recently and the conversation turned to amusing incidents in her school. In an English lesson one day she asked the question, 'What is a female dog called?'

One of the smarter pupils immediately replied, 'A bitch'.

'That's right Shaun,' she said, 'a female dog is a bitch.'

'You're swearing miss,' shouted Michael from the back of the classroom.

'No I'm not,' Margaret insisted, 'it's all right to say 'bitch' sometimes.

'Now who can tell me what a male dog is called?'
Michael waved his hand frantically.
'Yes, Michael, you tell the class.'
'Bastard,' miss.

In the old days a stationmaster and his family often lived in a small flat above the railway station.

One such stationmaster appeared in the small debts court. He was charged with owing large sums of money to several businesses in town and now agreed to repayment of his debts with a fixed sum per week over a period of years. The magistrate caused some amusement in the public gallery when he said in his summing up. 'From now on Mr. Munro you will do your utmost to keep out of debt. A man like you shouldn't be living above your station.'

The weekly court reports in *The Orcadian* rarely make exciting news. Many years ago I can remember one that caught my eye for its complete originality. It read:-

> *The accused was apprehended standing in the garden holding an*
> *Orkney cheese.*

I cannot remember the circumstances or the outcome but I have in my mind's eye a vivid picture of the accused in this happy position as if he were posing for a photograph.

Had *The Orcadian* existed in the 17th. century it would have had some exciting court proceedings to report. In those days parish courts still existed and they had extraordinary - and indeed cruel - powers. The parish worthies of Orphir were getting pretty fed up of a Liddle family who were found guilty for a second time of sheep stealing. What was particularly upsetting was that the family did not come from Orphir - they came into the parish only to steal sheep! I cannot remember how they were punished but I can recall that they were ordered to leave the parish immediately and the magistrate warned them that if they ever came into the parish again and committed such a crime they would have their feet cut off. The magistrate seemingly did not give much thought to the threat he issued. If he had had the Liddles' feet amputated, the parish would have been stuck with them!

Granny asked her little grand-daughter whether she had enjoyed her first week at school. 'No!' she replied emphatically, 'I couldna read and I couldna write, I couldna even spaek!'

It was September 3rd. 1939 and a bonny day in Stromness. A man walking along to the North End saw the blacksmith outside his smithy.

'Hi beuy,' he said by way of conversation, 'dae yi ken the 2nd. World War's broken oot.'

The blacksmith looked at the sky, 'Weel,' he says, 'thir gotten a grand day for hid.'

When I was a pupil at Stromness Academy the senior boys were given a great privilege; we were permitted to play basketball in the gym at lunchtime. With no teachers present we felt quite uninhibited in our use of language in the heat of a game. On one occasion a pupil crashed to the floor near the entrance to the gym as a result of rather a boisterous tackle and uttered a volley of oaths. As he lay there he was a bit shocked to notice a pair of black polished shoes right in front of his nose. He raised his head slowly to see the Rector frowning severely down at him.

'What was that Spence?' (we'll call him)

'Foul sir.'

'That is a perfect description of your language boy – come along with me!' And that ended the senior boys' privileges!

Another story from Stromness Academy in the 1950s. We were having a French lesson in the Vth. Form and the class was translating a story from French into English. The French verb *faire* is 'to do' but in some other instances it takes a different meaning. Jean was translating a paragraph which included the sentence *les voleurs sont allés faire leur affaire dans la forêt* which should have been translated 'the robbers went off to settle their business in the wood'. Jean had a different interpretation. Much to the amusement of everyone Jean chose to give the literal translation, 'the robbers went off to do their business in the wood'!

We had been doing a project on 'Fire' in Stenness Primary School. I ended the study by talking about the dangers of fire and the precautions we take to prevent it. By coincidence in English I had been reading to the class some of the strange epitaphs found on gravestones such as for example:-

Here lies my wife
Something her tongue never did

I thought that a good way to end the project would be to ask the pupils to draw the gravestone of someone who had done something stupid with fire and write a suitable epitaph on it. This was the clever epitaph that resulted in one case:-

Here lies the body of Mary Moar
Who set her house of Mire on fire
And burned it to the floor
There's no Moar there no more.

Granny was ironing. Fiona, her grand-daughter was drawing at the table but was having a good look at granny from time to time.

'Hoo owld are you granny?' she asked.

'Ah'm no tellan,' said granny.

'I ken a wey o findan oot,' Fiona persisted.

'Whit wey?' asked granny.

Fiona jumped up from her chair, went behind granny and started to pull at the top of her skirt.

'Whit are yi deuan bairn?' she asked.

'Weel hid says Age 5 to 6 on the band o me knickers and Ah'm gan tae see whit's on yirs!

An Orcadian who had been dabbling in spiritualism met an old friend. 'I wis spaekan tae yir fither the ither night min, ' he said.

Though the friend knew of the man's interest in spiritualism he was a little taken aback by this since his father had been dead for fifteen years.

After a moment's hesitation the friend blurted out, 'And hoo's he keepan?'

'Oh he's fine min. I spaek tae him a lot. In fact when Ah'm tryan tae spaek tae ither eens he keeps buttan in.'

The friend's confidence grew, 'Oh me fither wis aalwis like that,' he said!

In England two centuries ago a man came home from a morning's shooting, laid his gun on the table and fell asleep. By misfortune he laid his gun beside a goldfish bowl. After a time the sun's rays fell on the bowl which acted as a magnifying glass concentrating the sun's rays on the powder in the breech of the loaded gun. The powder exploded and the shot was driven out, killing the man.

At least two similar incidents have occurred in Orkney though with less disastrous results.

A lady told me that it was a Thursday, a bright sunny summer's day, and she had driven from the outskirts of Kirkwall into town to get a few messages. She parked her car and went first to get *The Orcadian*. She took it back to the car, sat in the driving seat for a little while scanning through it then deciding that she would have to get the rest of her messages done quickly she laid *The Orcadian* and her glasses on the passenger seat and went off. She didn't intend to be very long – but you know what it's like in Kirkwall – you meet one person after another whom you know, you make little progress and what would normally take ten minutes extends to half and hour or more. Eventually she got back to the car, opened the door and immediately smelt smoke. *The Orcadian* was blazing on the passenger seat! Going round to the passenger door she grabbed the paper and threw it outside – and with it went her glasses. Speaking to her man about the incident he thought rightly that her reading glasses which had thick lenses had acted as a magnifying glass and had set the paper on fire. As she said, 'Hid wis a mercy I didna meet anybody else on the street that I kent!'

A similar happening occurred when our family lived at Moorside, at the end of the Harray road. When I was a teenager I was standing outside the house with my mother, again on a bright sunny day. For some unexplained reason I looked at the sitting room curtains and saw strange black marks on them.

'Whit's that marks on the coorteens?' I asked my mother.

'I don't ken,' she replied, 'Ah'm niver seen that afore.'

'That marks are gittan bigger!' I said.

I went to have a closer look. 'The coorteens are on fire!' I shouted.

We dashed in and sure enough the curtains were blazing right up to the ceiling. I grabbed hold of the hems and with all my strength tore the curtains down, threw them on the floor and stamped out the fire.

And the cause of the fire? We had a little plastic ball in the window - a cheap Christmas ornament with a Santa in it. When the ball was shaken, snow began to fall over Santa! It too had acted as a magnifying glass setting the curtains on fire and so Santa was promptly consigned to the bruck quarry!

The verb 'hurl' in English means to 'throw'. In Orkney dialect one of its meanings is 'to give a lift to', e.g. a parent might give his child a hurl in a barrow.

Outside Leonard's shop in the war-time a newspaper hoarding read:-
ENEMY HURLED BACK FROM THE FRONT
An old fellow stood for some time absorbing the headlines then he grabbed a passer by and drew his attention to it. Pointing at the hoarding he said, 'Enemy hurled back fae the front indeed - I wad made the b-gg-rs waalk!'

It is often difficult to share jokes with foreigners. Apart from problems in translation they often have a completely different sense of humour. Nevertheless we can all enjoy the Germans' jokes about the 'simplicity' of the Friesian islanders. In this instance father, mother and their young son come to the big city of Berlin and marvel at the things they see. They go into an hotel for lunch. Mother is reading the menu on the wall while father and son walk round the imposing entrance hall. Suddenly they are surprised to see a very ugly woman open the door of a wall cupboard, go inside and close the door behind her. They don't know that it is a lift. A minute later the door opens and an absolutely beautiful woman comes out. Father turns to his son, 'Run and tell Mamma to forget about lunch - she must go into that cupboard next.'

A sooth country family moved into Stenness and the mother arrived at school early one morning to admit her young son. This gave me a good opportunity to talk to the pupil on his own. He had brought with him from his previous school several exercise books to give me some kind of idea of the standard of his work. As I flicked through them I said, 'Did you like your last teacher Gordon? (we'll call him)'

'Yes,' he replied, 'I liked her very much.'

'What did you like most about her?' I asked.

'She smelt so nice,' he replied.

'Do you think it would be a good idea if we had her on our staff?' I asked him.

'Yes,' he replied, 'I would like that.'

'So would I,' I said!

In the old days Orkney County Council workers were well known for their easy going approach. However they didn't get paid very well. Whether they didn't get much pay because they didn't work hard or whether they didn't work hard because they didn't get much pay no one knows but everyone knows they didn't work hard! Several council workers were ditching in Harray when along the road came a young farm worker leading a very difficult, flighty horse.

They laughed at the futile efforts of the farm hand to control the animal. Eventually one shouted, 'Watch yi don' t brak the neck o that horse beuy!'

But the farm worker was as smart. He shouted back, 'Thir's no much faer anyway o you brakkan the handle o that bloody shovel!'

A similar story comes from the North Isles where the job of roadman, especially on the smaller islands, was often a part-time post. Dave had been filling in pot-holes on the road in Wyre and was sitting in the ditch having a smoke when the postman came along.

'Er thoo workan on the roads the day Deevo?' he asked.

'I am,' replied Dave.

'I thowt thoo wir min,' remarked the postman, 'whin I saa thee sittan in the ditch.'

When I am out of Orkney my ears very quickly identify an Orcadian voice. In a busy Bournemouth store in the summer time some years ago I was forcing my way through the crowd to the door when two girls brushed past me going in the opposite direction. Just as they passed, one said to the other, 'Hid's doon at the buddum end.' I turned round and went after them but I lost them completely in the crowd. I wonder who they were?

As a teacher in training I was searching for a book in the library of Aberdeen College of Education. Suddenly I heard a voice at the other side of the shelves say 'Oh gaad!'

'Must be Orcadian,' I thought. I peeped round the corner and sure enough there was a Harray lass.

I told her how I had been able to identify her. 'Ah'll need tae keep me mooth shut,' she said, but knowing her well she wouldn't have found that very easy!

It is so easy to choose inappropriate language to express one's desires or feelings. Like a writer who, at great pains to describe the death throes of his hero totally destroyed the imagery by saying '......his breath came in short pants'!

An Orkney farmer tells the story of a terrible blunder made by his wife. Both went into a well-known Kirkwall furnishers where his wife wanted to buy a good, solid armchair. The assistant showed her a great variety of different types of chair all of which she tried but none seemed to satisfy her. Either the back wasn't the right angle or the seat was too long and made her legs stick out. The patient salesman in despair said to the wife, 'Whit exactly is the kind o chair that yi want; describe hid tae me.'

'The kind o chair I want,' she said, 'is a chair that'll grip me in aal the right pieces.'

This was too much for the salesman who roared and laughed and sought some reassurance, 'We are spaekan aboot a chair here are we no?' he asked!

When children learn material orally whether it be a song, a prayer or a poem they often subconsciously interpret any strange word or phrase in terms of their own experience. For instance when I was a little boy 'Home on the Range' was a popular song and I would proudly sing a verse or two if called upon to do so. However the word 'antelope' meant nothing to me. The word 'auntie' did and so my version of the song went 'where the deer and the auntie lo play.' It was only when someone in the family asked me what 'lo play' meant that I was stuck!

As an infant in a Roman Catholic school my wife had many prayers to learn orally. The word 'amongst' was unknown to her so during her first year in school instead of saying 'Blessed are thou amongst women' her version was 'Blessed are thou among swimming.'!

A Glasgow infant teacher felt that some of the children did not properly understand parts of the psalm, 'The Lord's my Shepherd'. She listened carefully to each child in turn. 'In pastures green he leadeth me' meant nothing to one child who had substituted the much more meaningful 'in past oor green he leadeth me'!

A primary school teacher asked her class to write out the Lord's prayer. One child in her class began the prayer in this way:- 'Eyes closed, hands together, not too fast and not too slow. Our father.......!

An Orkney wife on a journey north on the train formed the impression that the couple several seats in front were also islanders. She thought she could just hear the odd Orkney vowel here and there. The couple had a young boy with them who was not particularly well behaved. He was jumping up and down on the seat, and making funny faces at the passengers in the seats behind.

Suddenly the Orkney traveller got complete confirmation that the family was Orcadian when the mother called out in a loud voice to her son, 'Sit doon beuy or Ah'll gae yi a crack!'

I have spoken earlier about the very much higher incidence of swearing among the young today. When I was a pupil at primary school it was practically unknown, perhaps because the punishment for being caught was so humiliating. I can recall an older boy who had been caught swearing being led into a room in which there was a sink. The teacher took a scrubbing brush, dipped it in hot water and rubbed red Lifebuoy soap into the bristles until they were foaming. The boy was then forced to open his mouth and stick out his tongue whereupon she scrubbed his tongue hard with the soapy brush!

Of course there has always been swearing among adults and some Orkney men if they were alive today would surely come close to an entry in the Guinness Book of Records as the world's worst swearers.

In my student days I worked for long periods with the Orkney Builders.

When I told my brother where my first job was to be he said he knew the foreman there who would frighten me with his bad language. I was prepared for the worst but his first volley knocked me backwards. It had been a terrible weekend of wind and rain and when he came into the workmen's hut he chose to describe the weekend weather, the encrypted form of which is 'H..'s b....rd. bells, hid f...... weel lashed and p..shed ower the weekend; b....rd. h....ish'. His whole conversations were in the same vein; he even broke up words and put swear words in the middle. He didn't call a spade a spade - he put certain embellishments on it! Despite this, what a fine foreman he was. Poor Geordie (we'll call him) is no longer with us alas. Hard drinkers die of cirrhosis of the liver; I don't know what persistent swearing does to one's organs - perhaps cirrhosis of the speech lobes. Whatever it is, Geordie must have died of it.

Orkney and Shetland are the only remaining parts of Britain where 'thoo' and 'thee' are still used in the English language. At one time both Orcadians and Shetlanders used the form 'doo' and 'dee' but this form is found only in Shetland today. An amusing story from Harray, remembered for its fine alliteration and passed down through the generations, reminds us that at one time Orcadians used such forms too.

Two old eccentric Harray sisters lived on their own in the 19th century and a visitor called to see them. As the sisters were walking towards the door with their visitor a pigeon flew up out of the garden.

'Dat's me doo,' said the one.

But the other contradicted her, 'A doreen on dee Dora, dat's no dee doo, dee doo deed.' (Confound you Dora, that's not your pigeon, your pigeon died!)

Can you remember from your school days what a 'malapropism' is? The word comes from Mrs. Malaprop in Sheridan's play *The Rivals*. She often chose an out of place word to describe something when she was talking - like the Stenness wife who described somebody as being in the 'DDT's wi drink' or the Deerness man who in the 70s said he was going to buy an Austin Alligator. Then there was the Stronsay wife who talked about her neighbour who had such bad constipation that she had to be flown into hospital by Loganair for an anemone. A Kirkwall lady spoke of a fine Mary Alice which she had blooming in her ben end. This puzzled the listener until an amaryllis was produced. Perhaps the funniest malapropism I ever heard was a woman whose niece had graduated and now intended to take a year out, going to Israel to work in a kebab.

In the '50s a Kirkwall shopkeeper always carried away first prize for his geraniums and he used to taunt the old dears who competed with him by displaying his prize-winning entry in his shop. One day such a lady came in, took one look at the flowers and said, 'Me gerrydandrum wis far better as that.' From that day onwards his family always referred to such flowers as gerrydandrums!

I was at a concert in Stenness in the 70s where a farmer performed brilliantly on the tin whistle. After a long and intricate piece he stopped and said, 'Noo we'll hiv a short intromission while I get rid o the slaivers.' He shook the instrument and a long silver thread flew in the direction of the audience!

At one time tinkers were very much part of the rural scene in Orkney. They would pitch their tents on small pieces of common land, stay for a short while, leave at the spot a coded signal for their fellow travellers and move on.

One of the Firth ministers visited tinkers encamped on the old Market Green in Firth, now the site of the Community Centre.

He engaged in conversation with the father talking about one thing and another. Eventually the topic turned to religious matters and the minister pointed out the value of prayer to improve one's condition.

'Can you say a prayer Willie?' he asked.

Willie replied with his own question, 'Can you mak a tin pail boy?'

'I have to confess I can't,' said the minister.

'Weel,' said the tinker, 'every man tae his own trade.'

Just in case the reader hasn't heard it before, one of the best tongue twisters I have ever heard concerns a visitor to a tinker's encampment.

He watches the tinker at work for some time.

'Are you copper bottoming him?' the visitor asks.

'No, I'm aluminiuming him,' was the reply.

Try repeating the different possibilities for the bottom!

These tinkers were really hardy. One of their favourite stops was a piece of common land in Marwick below the cottage known as 'Hundland'. It was a cold and dark winter's morning about half past seven and a farmer was just going out with a storm lantern to attend to his kye when out of the darkness a figure approached him. It was a tinker from the encampment.

'I winder if you could spare a basin o hot watter boy for the wife's hivan a bairn.'

The farmer obliged.

Shortly afterwards the basin was returned and the farmer thanked. The tinker said that his wife had had a boy.

Looking out through his window at dinner time the farmer noticed that the tinkers were on their way again with the wife leading the pony!

Tinkers are recorded in Orkney as early as the 17th century. A good number of them arrived in Orkney in the middle of the 19th century 'Nolan', or as it was pronounced 'Nowlan', being a typical tinker name. Relations between Orcadians and tinkers were generally very good. They were often permitted to shelter in barns and outhouses in severe weather; the farmer would give a sheaf for the pony and the wife provide some bannocks and cheese if she believed that the family was in need. Of course bannocks were normally baked at the camp over an open fire but it must have been so difficult after a week of wind and rain.

One day a tinker wife came to Layburn in Rendall. They didn't like to beg openly so she told an unlikely tale.

'I was going tae bake lass but when I came tae look for the soda, I couldna find any. Robbie's dog's eaten a' wir bakin soda. Could ye spare a grain?'

Granny, tough old character that she was, could identify with the plight of the tinkers. She gave her some baking soda and some bannocks as well!

Stringent conditions apply today in all food manufacturing processes and quite right too for things were rather lax in the old days.

Before the war an Orphir wife was slicing a loaf and found a little dark circle in the middle of the slice. Peering closely she could not make out what it was. There was a similar dark circle in the main body of the loaf. Further cutting revealed the complete body of a mouse lying longitudinally in the loaf! With her first slice she had cut off the mouse's nose!

As a student in the early 1960s I worked at the Cheese Factory in Kirkwall. One of the workers who had been there since the factory opened told me that the manager had been very angry with the workers there one day. I'll let him describe what happened.

'Beuy he wis right mad and hid his aal tin intae the office. Seemingly a piece o cheese hid been sent back fae some piece in England. A wife hid fund a Players fag packet in hid!'

Despite uncompromising attention to hygiene, mistakes can still be made.

At Stenness School meals were not cooked on the premises; they were always brought in from another school. On one occasion a pupil came out and complained.

'The tatties taste o soap, sir.'

I never responded quickly to criticisms of school meals. 'I'll wait to see whether anyone else has a similar complaint, John,' I said and carried on with my work.

However it wasn't very long before another pupil came out and yet another and it was only when a white faced pupil came out foaming at the mouth that I decided some action was needed.

I went to Mary the dinner lady and passed on the pupils' observations.

'Yaas,' she said, 'the bairns are been complaining tae me too.'

The outcome was that none of the pupils ate any of the potatoes and I assured them that I would pass on my concern to the school kitchen which had prepared the meal. However I did not realise at the time that I would have such concrete evidence to support the pupils ' complaints.

At the end of the meal a pupil came to me to say that Mary wanted to see me immediately. I went along to our school kitchen and met her in the doorway.

'Ah'm just emptied oot the tattie pot and see whit I fand in the buddum,' she said.

I peeped into the big pot. There lay a large bar of green half melted, squelchy Fairy Soap! I apologised to the pupils telling them that whereas some folk had a fairy at the bottom of their gardens, we had a fairy at the buddum o wir tattie pot!

Some years ago I was crossing over to Rousay with the ferry. It was a beautiful summer's day and I spent the whole journey leaning over the railing yarnan to a weel kent Kirkwall man of Rousay extraction.

As we came into the Rousay pier he pointed to the shoreline and said, 'Whit a fine sight beuy Grigger - choldros and charlies.'

I strained my eyes. Yes I could see the choldros - the oystercatchers - but where were the charlies? Was this was a new Orkney bird name I had never heard of? Perhaps an old Rousay word.

'Whar's the charlies beuy?' I asked.

'Up abeun min on the bank,' came the reply.

'Whar?' I asked.

'There!' he said, pointing.

He was right. There on the bank were six grazing Charollais!

My brother Sandy took up the sport of hammer throwing when he was in his early twenties and he became an expert, his supreme achievement being invited to take part in an athletics tournament in Edinburgh. He prac-tised regularly every night on the base of an old army nissen hut which lay quite near the road but after a what could have been a disastrous acci-dent he chose another pitch. It happened in this way . To throw the hammer a hammer thrower spins round very fast within a circle before he releases it. It is very important to get the body movement synchronised with the swing of the hammer otherwise the hammer is liable to go off in any direction which is why the hammer thrower always operates with nets partly around him. Of course Sandy had no nets and on one occasion when his swing became very erratic, to prevent himself crashing on to the concrete base he let the hammer go. Unfortunately just at that time Nicholson's bus was passing and the hammer just missed the windscreen.

At the height of his athletic career in the 1960s brother Sandy went to Iran as an electrical transmission engineer. When on leave he flew home by Swissair which entailed an overnight stop in Switzerland. Suddenly Sandy realised that he might be able to achieve a boyhood dream of climbing the Matterhorn. He took himself to Zermatt and enquired about the possibility of finding a guide. In this he was successful. The guide looked him up and down and asked, 'Have you any mountain climbing experience?' Sandy had no option but to say, 'Yes' otherwise he knew that the guide would not accompany him. 'What was the last mountain you climbed?' the guide continued. Sandy jokingly replied, 'The Ward of Redland' (a 600 foot hill in Orkney). 'Where is that?' the guide persisted. 'It's in Scotland,' Sandy replied. The guide's face lit up, 'Ah, you are a Scottish mountaineer - then we can do business.' To cut a long story short, Sandy hired equipment, climbed the Matterhorn and brought back photographs to prove it but he said it was quite a frightening experience. He said that when he got back to base he thanked the guide and told him that that was the second time he had climbed the Matterhorn. The guide was a bit perplexed. 'The second time?' he asked. 'Yes,' Sandy replied, 'the first and the last'! Today, with expert gear and guide ropes, 3000 people a year climb Matterhorn!

An acquaintance and his wife went on an African safari and regularly stayed in safari camps in the middle of the bush. On one occasion in the middle of the night he heard a scream and woke up to find that his wife was not beside him. He grabbed a torch and dashed out of the room. She was in the corridor in a state of shock. And the explanation? She had been sitting on the toilet when something had jumped up at her. Her husband shone the torch into the toilet and saw reflected in the light the eyes of a big African frog!

This story illustrates the importance of learning a foreign language. One morning a Stenness farmer was having a morning cup of coffee when the 'phone rang. It was his neighbour who had rung to tell him that his bull had broken down the fence and was out on the main road. Davie (we'll call him) rushed out to find that the bull had in fact escaped and had taken up a position in a bus shelter, head down and snorting! He immediately realised that he would have to stop traffic on the road. Looking to his left he saw what he feared most - coming along the road at a casual pace was a cyclist, clearly a foreign tourist. As the cyclist approached Davie shouted, 'Waatch oot min - thir's a bull at the bus stop.' The tourist raised his hand, gave a friendly wave and spoke what was probably the only words he knew, 'Good morning sir' and cycled on. All of a sudden he saw the bull and such was his acceleration that the farmer said he could hear the crunching of the chain! Clearly it wasn't a Spanish tourist!

A Kirkwall lass, a student, went on holiday to the south of France with an English classmate. One afternoon both were enjoying the Mediterranean sunshine on the beach. In such an environment they felt quite uninhibited; they removed their bikini tops and sat there for some time soaking up the sunshine and watching holidaymakers passing to and fro on the beach, no one paying any attention to them for such a thing was commonplace. However the afternoon became rather hot and they decided that they had better use some sun screen. Both were liberally applying sun tan lotion when all of a sudden the Kirkwall lass screamed and covered herself with a towel.
'What's wrong Kerry? What's wrong?' her friend called out anxiously. She immediately thought that Kerry had been stung by a wasp.
Kerry peeped gingerly out from underneath her towel, 'Ah'm just seen a Kirkwall man go by,' she said!
Kerry by the way is not her correct name! It is uncertain whether the man saw Kerry, probably not, but what would he have said had he seen her? 'Grand day!' would seem to have been inappropriate in the circumstances. Old folks would have said, 'Bra day!' but that wouldn't have been very fitting either!

I hadn't seen Stevie for a number of years and when I met him in the street recently he was hirplan.
'My whit's happened thee?', I asked.
'Oh I wis takkan this five gallon drum o oil oot o the boot o the car beuy - a thing Ah'm done many's the time and me back gid and that wis that and than I gid doon wi sciatica. That is a most painfil thing beuy. Me leg's nivver been right since an that's twa 'ear ago.'
I sympathised wi Stevie and asked him if he had seen the doctor.

'The doctor!' he said in despair, 'I speired him whit wis really wrong wi me leg an he said hid wis just me age. Feth that pat me mad fur as I tellt him – the tither leg is the sam age an thir's noatheen wrong wi har'!

Stromness WRI held a competition – as SWRIs do! Each married woman had to bring up a childhood photograph of her man and attach to it a little piece of poetry to provide a slight clue to his identity. One of the Stromness ladies approached me to help her with a verse. She thought that if I included something about jogging in the poem it would supply the clue that was required. Her man happened to be an old school friend and I was pleased to be able to be given an opportunity to pull his leg! Here is the poem (with apologies to William Wordsworth)

> *As lonely as a clood I jog*
> *Ower Brenkie's, doon by Dale*
> *Me trusty trainers tread the turf*
> *Faered for nither rain nor gale.*
> *Onward ploddan, pechan, ploutan*
> *Drivan me body tae hids limit*
> *Swaetan like a bull I run*
> *Wi sabbid shorts and sark and semmit.*
> *Me legs are gittan kinda weefly*
> *At last I see the lights o home*
> *Am I gan tae mak hid this time?*
> *Ah'm waek as watter, fairly doan.*
> *The last few steps I craal exhausted*
> *And slump against wir gairdeen fence*
> *And ask mesael the sam owld question*
> *'When will I ever learn some sense?'!*

We had a real concert pianist in Stenness School one day. The teachers briefed their classes on the visit and carefully went over some of the questions which could be asked at the end stressing that they should be related to music. Having vetted them all and eliminated quite a few, the performance went ahead.

At the end the pianist stood up, was applauded and asked, 'Now have you any questions to ask about me or my work?'

One of the youngest pupils stood up and said, 'Please sir, dae yi hiv any girlfriends?' The teachers' toes curled up in embarrassment! However the pianist rose to the occasion and provided the perfect answer in terms of his brief to talk about music.

'My dear,' he said, 'I practise the piano for seven hours every day; how can I have time for girlfriends?'

An English tourist in Westray developed a high temperature and the bed and breakfast lady was rather concerned about her welfare. She insisted that her guest go to bed immediately but the suggested 'cure' rather surprised the visitor.

'Ah'll mak a hot watter bottle tae yi,' she said, 'just you go tae bed right awey and pit yir head on a big cod and yi'll be aalright.'

I always picture this in my mind especially since Westray is well known for its fishing industry! A cod is of course a pillow!

Between languages it can be understood that even more ambiguities occur. An English firm of perfumers produced a body spray called SNO-MIST. When it came to export sales they found that sales in Sweden were nil. None of the wholesalers would buy it. A salesman asked a Swedish importer if he knew the reason for this.

The Swede laughed, 'Maybe a good product,' he said, 'and a fine sounding name in English but in Swedish it means 'snake dung'.

Accidents never come singly they say and when one accident follows another in quick succession, it can send us reeling. A Kirkwall mother was sitting quietly reading the paper when the telephone rang. It was the police to say that her thirteen year old son Ronald had been knocked off his bicycle and was in Balfour Hospital unconscious.

'Queek!' she said to her ten year old son Alistair, 'Ronald's been in a accident - get in the car and we'll drive tae the 'ospital.'

When they came into the ward mother saw to her great relief that though Ronald was badly cut about the face, he was sitting up in bed.

While she was talking to him and comforting him there was a crash behind her. She looked round to see her son Alistair slumped on the floor. Nurses came running to see what had happened. Alistair was lying unconscious. He had fainted with the shock of seeing Ronald and as he had fallen his head had hit the steelwork of a bed. He was undressed and put in an empty bed next to his brother! We can all imagine how the mother felt!

A Dounby School teacher had a free period. Going into the staffroom she was desperate for a cup of tea. But would you believe her bad luck; there was not one tea-bag in the school kitty. But she had to have to have a cup of tea! What could she do? Then she remembered that some of the visiting teachers brought their own tea with them and left it in the school rather than use out of the school kitty. Had they by any chance left any tea? Her luck was in. There was a small packet at the back of the cupboard and inside were a dozen or so tea bags. Acting on the old Orkney principle that nobody ever misses a sook fae a coo, she took a tea bag, popped it into a cup, boiled the kettle and waited. Soon she was pouring the hot water into the cup and after another little wait in went the milk – and then to savour that lovely refreshing cup of tea!

She took one mouthful and ran to the sink. It was an absolutely diabolical taste.

'Ah'm niver tasted such terrible tea in me life,' she said to herself, 'hid must be as owld as the hills. There's only wan piece for that packet o tea, and that's in the dustbin.' And that's where all the tea went.

Some days later at break time all the teachers, including visiting teachers were in the staffroom. Suddenly the teacher heard an English voice say, 'Anyone seen my tea? I'm sure I left it at the back of the cupboard here where no one would find it. Anyone seen my tea?'

Some teachers joined in the search but there was no tea to be found. 'Must have been cleaned out by mistake,' said one of the teachers. 'Sorry about that, have a cup of our tea,'

'Oh, I couldn't drink that disgusting stuff!' he said, 'thanks all the same. But I am disappointed about my tea. It was the last of a fine consignment of Earl Grey which I had specially sent from Harrod's.'

The teacher concerned kept her head down marking books.

'My,' she said afterwards, 'I wis black affronted!'

Listening is a skill. 'Learn to listen,' says the teacher, 'then listen to learn.' But some folk <u>don't</u> listen! I feel really annoyed if I'm telling somebody something and I know they are not listening. Here is a good example of this – it also happens to be about the same brand of tea and it makes a good story into the bargain.

An old Rousay man had been to visit an English family who had moved into a nearby house. He was telling a neebor wife about his visit.

'I hidna been in very long till they asked me wir I wantan a cup o tea.'

'Oh yaas,' I said, 'I wid hiv a cup o tea. And than they speired me if I wanted Earl Haig's tea. Oh, hid wad deu me fine I said I can drink any kind o tea. Weel this tea they gid me lass, I couldna drink hid. Terrible taste wi hid. Are yi ever heard o Earl Haig's tea?'

'Are yi sure hid wisna Earl Grey tea that they offered yi?'

'O, best kens, bit if yi ever go tae that hoose and they ask yi if yi want Earl Haig's tea, for mercy sake say no. Hid's enough tae pit yi aff tea aal-taegither.'

I was proudly showing a German friend around Orkney. We were travelling through South Ronaldsay and the friend remarked on how strong the stone-built buildings seemed.

'Oh yes,' I replied, 'very strong; they would stand for hundreds of years.'

When we turned the next corner we both burst out laughing. Right in front of us was an old barn, one end of which had totally collapsed!

Two men had been lending a hand with the neighbour's crop on North Ronaldsay and afterwards they were invited in for supper. Set in front of them was smoked fish which had been cooked in milk. It was served in soup plates with an over- generous supply of milk in which it had been prepared.

On the way home one said to the other, 'Whit did thoo think o that fish beuy?'

The other pondered for a bit, 'Dammit min hid wis aal right whin I catched hid.'

An English lady who had taken up residence in Orkney told a neighbour that she would like to try some typical old Orkney dishes. The neighbour suggested among other things, salt fish and boiled tatties with a bit of melted butter. Some weeks later the neighbour enquired whether she had tried any of the dishes she had suggested. She replied that she had only tried the salt fish so far and that she hadn't enjoyed it; in fact she couldn't eat it at all. When the neighbour enquired further it became apparent that the lady had fried the salt fish directly! In Italy they actually do fry salt fish but they boil it and drain the water several times first!

If you want to know how to get round a North Ronaldsay man, read on....

All the elders of the North Ronaldsay kirk were present to hear a candidate for the vacant post of minister take the Sunday service. After the service was over there were muted whispers among the elders, all agreeing that the candidate had conducted a poor service and had delivered a most disappointing sermon. However in the time honoured tradition the candidate was invited to the manse where the ladies of the congregation had prepared tea in the sitting room. The company had just taken their seats in front of a roaring fire when the candidate surprised everyone by opening his briefcase and taking out a bottle of whisky. He pulled out the cork and threw it on the fire. Half a dozen glasses were brought at his request by one of the ladies, generous measures were poured and glasses refilled until at last the bottle was empty.

On the way home one of the elders said to the other, 'Ah'm tinkan he's no seek a ill fulloo as we towt.'

When a Norwegian fishing boat anchored off Wyre, Davie, a local man thought he would row out and investigate. He asked to speak to the skipper. After some time the skipper appeared and leaned over the railings.

'Does thoo spaek English?' Davie enquired.

'Yes,' the skipper replied in crisp tones, 'but you don't'!

I learned Norwegian for a year and when I went to Norway I spoke haltingly in that language. I soon learned that this was not necessary for most Norwegians spoke impeccable English. This reminds me about a trip my brother made to Sweden on business. Landing at Stockholm airport he took a taxi into the city and engaged the driver in conversation. My brother knew no word of Swedish and was not one to change his normal way of speaking Orcadian and substitute it by chanting. After every remark my brother made, the taxi driver asked him to repeat it. In the end the taxi driver, despairing, said, 'I have never before met anyone who speaks such bad English'!

A Kirkwall man used to tell the story of an experience he had when he was a young boy. It was a lovely summer's day and this had attracted a number of children and parents down to the bay at Weyland. Evan really wanted to swim like the other children but he had no bathing trunks. After watching them for some time he decided to throw off his clothes and go in naked. He put his clothes in a little pile and placing his hands in a strategic position tip-toed gently over the gravel down to the sea. His path took him past a large and outspoken Kirkwall lady who as soon as she saw him called out, 'Oh no need tae worry aboot me seean hid Evan, Ah'm tin bigger things oot o a wilk wi a preen'!

'Moosewab' is an interesting old Orkney dialect word. It means 'cobweb' and entered our dialect from Scots where it was recorded as early as the 16th century. It must have referred originally not to the large circular webs which we often see but to the thick, grey web which we see between stones inside an old oothouse. The big spider leaves a hole in the web and pops in and out of the hole should it feel any tremor on the web. We used to have an outside toilet when we lived at Binscarth Cottages and as a very young child I can remember sitting on the bucket and teasing spiders to come out of their holes by tickling their web with a piece of paper! It is little wonder that the web was called a 'moosewab' since the spider behaves just like a little mouse.

An old verse from 19th century Orkney tells of a time when every-one went to the kirk and religion was uppermost in everyone's mind:

Jerusalem is a bonny piece,
Nae mouch (moth) or moosewab there,
Hids streets are laid wi baeten gold,
Oh gin I wis there!

Sadly Jerusalem today creates a different image in the mind.

There is a lovely old Orkney story about a moosewab and 'chantan' i.e. trying to 'spaek proper'. One day a lady from Sanday came into Kirkwall with her son to see Auntie Margaret. Auntie Margaret was ashamed of her North Isles farming roots which she associated with gutter and mess. She had become a proper Kirkwall lady who kept a spotlessly clean house and who shunned the use of dialect. Among themselves the Sanday family made fun of her but the boy was warned to be on his very best behaviour in Auntie's house. Auntie made them very welcome as usual and went through to the kitchen to make a cup of tea. The little boy sat quietly but teased his mother by drawing his finger over a highly polished side table to see if there was any dust on it. All of a sudden he pointed and exclaimed in rather a loud voice, 'Luk mither – there's a moosewab!' Unfortunately, just at that juncture Auntie entered, heard the remark and glared at the little boy. 'William,' she said, 'there is nothing like that in my house and more-over it isn't a moosewab, it's a cobweb'!

I think mother and William must have laughed all the way home to Sanday!

An English lady who was very religious frequently spent her summer holidays in Sanday. She became very friendly with a farmer and his wife and one day confided in them that she would really like to come and live permanently on the island. John and his wife gave her no encouragement to do this for as they told her, she would never be able to stand an Orkney winter. One summer she arrived at the door in a great state of excite-ment. She was warmly welcomed as usual and before she sat down exclaimed that she had made her mind up – she really was coming to live in Orkney.

John was not impressed. 'My whar are yi gan tae bide?' he asked.

'Oh, the good Lord has given me a caravan to live in,' she replied.

John was even less impressed. 'The good Lord is gin yi a caravan tae bide in is he? Feth come some coorse winter's night he'll mibbe tak hid awey again'!

. . . THERE'S NO MORE